UMW - 1979 - 81 9

D0670407

Why Joy?

learning to love my special child

Why Joy?

learning to love my special child

Jane Jennings

CHRISTIAN HERALD BOOKS
Chappaqua, New York

Prelude

TODAY IS IMPORTANT—vitally important to me. It is Joy's birthday, and she is happy. Happy! I want to shout my thanks to God. He gave us this special child. He gave us a seemingly insoluble problem, and then solved it. He answered the many "whys" that swirled in my mind, shrouding each day. The whirlpool of doubt tested my faltering faith in God, and it was not until I surrendered my problem to him that answers appeared. Joy is today living proof of the love and power of God.

Today is particularly important; it evokes memories of the day of her birth, thirty-four years ago. I wish we could watch as she opens the several gifts we sent her, each wrapped individually in bright paper and tied with fancy ribbons to delight her acute color-consciousness. She enjoys opening the packages as much now as on her third birthday.

It is unlikely she will ever finish knitting the sweater. She probably will start it immediately, after she reads the easy-to-follow instructions in the kit. If her interest lasts long enough, she may even knit and purl a few rows. Quite possibly she will rip it all out one day and begin anew. No matter. It will give her pleasure for a while.

5

The subscriptions to *Guideposts* and *Reader's Digest* will bring her a present each month. She likes mail. Receiving anything is somewhat a status symbol at the home where she lives and therefore even magazines are important to Joy.

I'd love to watch as she tries each crayon and identifies the color before using it in the coloring book. And I'd love to listen as she practices the new songs on her chord organ. She may work a few of the crossword puzzles in the book which one aunt and uncle sent, candidly completing each by referring to the answers at the back of the book.

Joy will have her own decorated cake and ice cream at the dinner table today, and the other girls will sing to her. She will be the center of attention—and love it! Then, at the end of the month, she and the others who also had April birthdays will celebrate at a joint party. If the day is warm enough the party may be held outdoors, as a group picnic. But inside or out, elaborate or plain, Joy will be pleased and happy. She will be included, not rejected; and her pleasure will be beautiful. How I wish I could be there and see her unusual eyes brighten with excitement, and listen as she chatters like a mockingbird—the way it was when she was a tiny little girl.

Joy's childlike reactions, mannerisms and behavior no longer worry me as they once did—before God took over. There are only a few subtle changes noticeable in her personality. Her actions are as variable and unpredictable as the weather. Her moods soar heavenward and then plunge hellward. Why? I don't know, but reasons are not important now. God knows.

Many of the other "whys" that once threatened us

have also waned in importance. What is pertinent is the fact that Joy is happy. She has friends and companionship and a job. She feels useful and needed. She is *Somebody* in her own sight. She accepts herself as she is, a person with a slight handicap.

She was not always happy. The depth of her frustration and misery became clear to me when I found a sheet of notebook paper in her desk one day after we placed her in a home-away-from-home. The paper was one of several blank sheets and "test papers" from her make-believe students. Joy had printed "The story of my life." It was brief—"Born: April 9, 1944. Died: " I don't know when she wrote it, but she was twenty-one when I discovered it.

All lingering doubts as to the wisdom of having placed Joy disappeared. That God works in mysterious ways was a proven fact.

For years I could not understand why he gave me the problems and Joy the handicap. Neither could I understand why he did not reveal to me an unsuspected ability to write, with no educational training or background. Now I am convinced that one "why" answered the other.

chapter *1*

WE HAVE a special child. She is handicapped. We had a problem that God solved.

My story began April 7, 1944.

The suitcase was packed and sitting near the front door. The refrigerator and cupboard were stocked for Jerry's convenience. The diaper service and practical nurse were "on alert." Everything was ready and waiting—even the crib and toiletries. Already ten days overdue, the child within me kicked and exercised but gave no sign of a readiness to break the umbilical moorings. Good Friday 1944 threatened to be another slow day of waiting.

It was a sunny spring day. Trees were greening and the dormant earth was poised for another surge of life. A few daffodils and narcissus were already waving a welcome to Easter. The more timid tulips poked their stubby snouts through the warm earth, not quite ready to brave blooming. Then, as the lazy hours yawned and stretched into late afternoon, dark clouds dulled the sun's brilliance and I shivered with the sudden chill. A storm seemed to be in the offing.

The thought of a storm depressed me, but Jerry dismissed my reaction as a side effect of my condition.

"Maybe tonight will be the time, Janey," he said. It was.

As he drove to the hospital late that night the wind howled and whined. Angry gusts set bare branches dancing and pirouetting like a band of whirling dervishes. A series of lightning bolts slashed the purple-black sky. A crescendo of thunderclaps, the steady hum of the motor and tires, and the frequent roar of the wind made an unpleasant, ugly song. The windshield wipers served as a metronome in the overall cacophony. Their rhythmic swish, swash, swish, swash still echo in my memory of the events preceding Joy's birth.

Time has blurred my recollection of many details, but not of that storm and the earlier beauty of Good Friday 1944. They are typical of Joy's personality—changeable and uncontrollable, angelic and demoniac, and always unpredictable. But Joy was not born that night. Instead she arrived Easter Sunday, April 9, 1944.

I have often heard that all women remember every minute detail surrounding the birth of their first child, but I recall almost nothing of what occurred after we arrived at the hospital near midnight Friday, until early Sunday morning.

Time began again as the anaesthetic wore off and consciousness gradually returned. I missed the almost perpetual movement in my body. The baby had been born! Son or daughter? It didn't matter. From far off, in a sort of grayed vacuum, I heard the obstetrician say, "You have a perfect little girl, Mrs. Jennings."

Then Jerry repeated that world-shaking sentence, as he leaned to kiss my forehead. "Janey, hey, Mother! We've got a perfect little girl! She's a doll—the tiniest little girl ever. All red, and no hair at all. But boy, can she yell!

Nothing wrong with her lungs, that's for sure."

He stroked my cheek and I reached for his hand, pulling his fingers to feel my emptiness; and he kissed me again. Then he left and I dozed, totally happy. We had an Easter child, he had said. And Jerry and I were parents, at long last.

The day and the whole wide world were bathed in beauty, but the joy of new motherhood put the brilliant sun to shade and the world's glow was the reflected radiance of my motherhood. The past ugliness of the storm was remote and unreal. Diamond droplets of rain sparkled on the sharp needles of a tall pine outside the hospital window, and then evaporated into nothingness. Sharply defined shadows streaked across the lawn, clear and dark. Shivering, I recalled that the brightest sun makes the darkest shade.

By grace I was the mother of a little girl. I mouthed the new title several times, savoring its full meaning. Then I practiced the sounds of "Mom," "Mama," and "Mommy," as if the names were original and unique to me. Now we could discard "it," and substitute "daughter." I wondered if Jerry was disappointed at having a girl instead of a boy. Perhaps the next, or the next, or. . . . She was *not* to be a "lonely only."

Worries ceased when a nurse carried my daughter to me, wrapped in a cocoon of blankets, and sound asleep. She was feminine and dainty, and unbelievably beautiful. How odd that I, Plain Jane, had given birth to a daughter destined to be a beauty queen. My cup of smugness overflowed and embarrassed me.

Holding her gingerly, I examined my exquisite child from bald pate to big toe. Two eyes and two ears, ten toes and ten fingers, and the tiniest feet imaginable. She was truly a six-pounds-and-four-ounces "bundle of joy," smelling faintly of baby powder. Her head was shaped perfectly and I wondered what color her hair would be. It was of no consequence, but she might be dark like Jerry or fair like me.

How odd it was to meet her for the first time. She had been the pivotal consideration in our lives all those long waiting months, a part of me, yet we were strangers. She didn't even have a name. But she was a person—and perfect! I felt most important.

Her tiny feet intrigued me and I kept them uncovered as I continued examining her. She nursed briefly and then fell asleep. This was my first experience, too; but it seemed she should have nursed longer. Also, she had spit up all over herself and me. I rang for the attendant, who shrugged off my concern. She commented that most new mothers are overly worried and fret needlessly, but she did show me how to tap those tiny feet and pinch her cheeks to keep my baby awake and nurse.

My daughter—I loved the words—soon fell asleep again, her fingers curled tightly around mine. How strong they were! Jerry would laugh at me if I were to tell him that she seemed to be holding onto me for security, on her first day of life. When the nurse returned for her, I carefully removed my finger, sad at having to part with my child.

I daydreamed. I saw her grow through infancy and school, college, and was planning her wedding gown when Jerry returned that afternoon, his arms loaded with Easter lilies and a huge box of chocolates. He was the picture of proud fatherhood, beaming and "bustin' his buttons."

We marveled again and again at our special child, planning for the future and using our new titles many times. He preferred "Daddy" to "Pop," and he agreed that our pride and joy should be named Joy.

In those days pride was our paramount emotion. Second best was not good enough for me or Jerry. We were the proudest parents one could ever imagine! (Later we learned that pride put a burden on us and Joy and everyone near us. That burden grew and grew, threatening to crush all of us.)

Joy's having spit up after nursing troubled me, so I insisted that Jerry check with the pediatrician. He cautioned me against being a worrywart and fussbudget on Day One. "Lots of babies never get anything but basic instinct rearing, Janey, and they survive. And those three baby books you have at home should have all the answers."

We were intense, vowing that nothing would be too expensive or rare for our exceptional daughter. Still, we must not sacrifice discipline and spoil her. We would never have a spoiled brat. Not our child. She would be a model of good behavior and manners. I would teach her to cook and sew and be a good housekeeper. We would attend Sunday school and church as a family. We would present her for christening as soon as I completed the fancy dress I'd been holding in abeyance in case we had a son. I put the boy's suit pattern away for the time being. Hopefully our next child would be a son.

We had much to learn. In the days at the hospital I asked many, many questions; and in the following years "why" became an overworked word in our vocabularies.

Surely all children were not so puzzling. It must be I

who was incompetent—an imperfect specimen of Mother at best.

Solicited and unsolicited advice from well-intentioned friends and relatives, and our own basic instinct failed to answer our many questions of Joy's behavior, health and development. We floundered, striving to cope with numerous inconsistencies. We grabbed at wisps of possible help, reading and rereading the three baby books and changing doctors frequently in our search for guidance and answers.

Joy's health was a mammoth worry. And the problems persisted. Two of the seven pediatricians who examined her suggested a vague allergy as the cause of her spitting up almost daily, and both treated the situation lightly. Joy continued to spit up without warning, day and night, awake and asleep. I marveled that she continued to gain weight and height.

Once, in her second year, after several days of frequent regurgitating, Joy was listless and wan; and the doctor hospitalized her for dehydration. Her weight was about halved by the siege. Jerry and I panicked, certain there was something radically wrong with Joy's digestive system. For two years we had asked and asked the same question but still had no answer. I prayed that the doctor would run tests in the hospital which would reveal the problem and a cure for her regurgitation and constipation.

Joy sobbed and whimpered much of the night as she lay quietly in the stark metal hospital crib, the life-sustaining liquid dripping into her body. Occasionally she struggled to remove the needle, but she did not cry. Perhaps she did not have the strength.

In a couple of days she was stronger and we took her

home to recuperate. The cause of the "viral infection" was still unknown, but Joy was back to her brand of normal behavior.

The doctor dismissed our concern for Joy's health and physical development. "You expect too much of her," he said. "Stop being perfectionists. You'll live longer."

The doctors had varying opinions, but all agreed the condition was temporary. I recalled that other pediatricians had assured us Joy would be fine when she was able to sit up alone. When the problem persisted, they had said it would take care of itself when she crawled; when she stood; when she walked; and then, when she ran. But Joy continued to vomit at any time of the day or night. It made social outings of all types touch-and-go. Church attendance became embarrassing and even unpleasant at times. And the laundry was always piled high, waiting for the weekend when we could use the facilities of a nearby laundromat.

Joy's digestive problems caused us so much concern that her physical slowness had lost some of its impact and had gone almost unnoticed. She was a bit behind in sitting unaided and did not walk alone until seventeen months. She crawled in a funny bumping-along manner. I wondered if her tiny feet made balancing difficult. She hated to wear shoes, and methodically untied every knot and unlaced the shoes, chewing the laces and shoes puppy fashion.

It puzzled us that Joy's feet did not keep pace with her legs' growth. According to the books, she was taller than average at age two; and if the projection was infallible, her thirty-eight inches would double to six-feet-four at maturity. Everyone in Jerry's family is tall but my people are short. We wondered what Joy's eventual height would be. A six-feet-four girl could have a lot of problems, we agreed.

Tall, medium, or short—we loved her. Our Joy was a beautiful child. Period. Her dark auburn hair reflected the sun and glowed with a thousand bronzed lights. It was thick and glossy, and exquisite when she sat still long enough for me to brush it. Her fair complexion was clear and luminous, and Joy and I spent long days outside in the summer so that the sun could embrace her and kiss color into her pale cheeks. She did not become as tanned as butterscotch pie, but a spattering of caramel-toned freckles added to her total prettiness.

Her hazel eyes fascinated me. They were unlike any others I had ever seen—almost transparent at times and opaque at others. They missed nothing. Nor did her ears. All of her senses were unusually well-honed.

Jerry and I were typical first-time parents, I suppose. We took roll after roll of photographs to record her development and Joy seemed to enjoy the procedure immensely. Our little peahen preened and postured in her new clothes, and several times would leave her pose to look in the mirror, mimick my makeup ritual and then return to have her picture taken.

Photographs and growth statistics and laboratory tests were concrete factors. The reasons for Joy's behavior were abstract. There were no guidelines to follow. Advice from relatives, friends, neighbors, books and doctors did not fit our situation. Prayers began to seem a waste of time, but habit kept me on my knees while Joy's actions kept me on my toes.

chapter 2

JOY'S FIRST two years were eventful. We were worried and oftentimes terrified. Our pride suffered and I was sometimes ashamed because of the many inconsistencies in Joy's behavior and development. They defied understanding and Joy fit no mold.

Frequently I had an eerie feeling that Joy was looking beyond me or through me toward some thing or some person at a far distant place. A "veil" dropped over her clear eyes, and she was "gone." I remember reading once that eyes are the mirror of the soul; but Joy's were unsilvered, reflecting nothing of her thoughts.

It was surprising to us that she missed nothing of what went on around her and that she memorized everything she saw or heard. We boasted and bragged about Joy's extensive vocabulary and her use of adult words with many syllables. She parroted our mealtimes grace and bedtime prayers. Nursery rhymes and songs by the dozens became part of her repertoire; and she repeated verbatim the words of books, page by page, before she was three years old. We wondered if she actually could read or if she had memorized the words. She recited jingles from radio commercials, and could direct a new babysitter to the exact location of her clothing, bedding, or food. She recognized landmarks; and one day when I took an unaccustomed route to the grocery she became most upset. She quieted only when we arrived at our familiar destination.

Both of us loved to show off Joy's capabilities, marveling at how she had identified items of food, from pumpkins to avocadoes and spaghetti, at age two. She could name many flowers and animals and spelled her name at two-and-a-half. She glibly counted anything and everything she saw. Numbers were obviously her strong point.

In spite of her linguistic ability she relied on gestures and grunts to get things she wanted instead of asking for them. One suggestion tossed my way was that Joy was lazy. Another, she knew she could convey her wishes wordlessly and was "dumb like a fox." One relative intimated that Joy was the dominant one in the family. Maybe she was right. If I insisted that Joy tell me what she wanted she either lost interest or became violently angry. The resulting confusion and frustration were not worth holding out for her verbalization. Being namby-pamby had merit!

Joy, too, was namby-pamby about many things. Much of the time she was content to sit quietly in a chair or on the floor, holding a soft, cuddly toy made of yarn or a terry cloth bib with which she tickled her nose. She studied the pictures on her big building blocks for long periods of time, but did not build anything. She was not an active child until I attempted to brush and braid her hair or mark the hem in a new dress. Then she wriggled and squirmed constantly. She seemed to enjoy wearing a ruffly dress and showing it to anyone who would look at it;

and the embroidered animals and flowers on pinafores or aprons or dresses were especially interesting to her. However, she persisted in picking out the stitches and tearing holes in all of her clothing.

Joy's destructive bent extended to herself. She picked at her toenails and fingernails and never let a scrape or cut heal normally. She has permanent scars on her face, legs, hands, and arms from tiny mosquito bites that developed into large and festering sores after she sat and dug at the itching stings while putting together the pieces of a jigsaw puzzle.

She loved puzzles and they were easy for her to assemble. She, herself, was the most confusing puzzle of all. I reread all three baby books and asked more questions. One book listed various toys geared to aid both large and small muscle development. Maybe they would interest her and she would not take such long afternoon naps or sleep until so late each morning.

I could barely wait for Christmas to come so that we could convert our small apartment to a muscle-building "toy shop." She had to be encouraged to do something! Perhaps she would play with the balls or a kiddie car instead of sitting in her high-low chair while I did my housework, listening to the stories I recited or singing with me or listening to her records.

Jerry and I were as excited as Joy when Santa Claus finally came for her third Christmas visit. She held the packages and then sat down on the floor to examine the wrappings. Joy made no effort to open any package until Jerry showed her what to do. Then she stared at the paper around each item before tearing the wrapping from her gifts. She did enjoy the fancy paper but none of the new toys had much impact. She rustled each piece and then tore it to shreds while squealing with delight. Jerry and I were dumbfounded when Joy soon lost all interest in the new toys, reached for her old yarn doll, and put her thumb in her mouth, ready for a nap.

We were equally amazed a couple of days later when Joy began to chatter about the jack-in-the-box and Santa Claus, both pictured on the wrappings. She even played with one of the large balls. She could not catch it if we threw it to her, so we rolled it her way. She picked it up with one hand and tossed it toward Jerry! Our spirits soared.

Joy ignored the kiddie car completely, nor did she push the wheeled toys except back and forth while sitting on the floor cuddling her tattered old yarn doll. Sometimes she held the new doll, but it would never replace her longtime favorite.

We had mixed emotions over Joy's reaction to the blocks. She did not stack them or build anything, but studied the pictures intently. Eventually she followed our lead and spelled simple words with the alphabet letters on the blocks. Spelling her name was easy and she took much time choosing the three letters to line up; forming J O Y, her name, on the blocks, fascinated her and she sat for long periods of time staring at the letters.

She appeared unable to cope with those three wooden objects as identifying her. They were J-O-Y, but *she* was Joy! What did that mean? Many times she knocked them flying while screaming in anger and frustration. Later, as she grew to school age, any usage of the word—as a sentiment or another girl's name—involved a stormy session of trying to explain the difference. I told her that she had brought so much joy to us that we had felt she should be named Joy, and that when we sang "Joy to the World!" at Christmastime it was because Christ's coming had brought wondrous things to all mankind. Joy meant happiness and pleasure. But joy had no meaning for her except as it identified our daughter. *She* was Joy!

In other areas Joy learned at a fast rate and it was impossible *not* to teach her the alphabet and number combinations. I hoped this would not present a problem of boredom when she entered school. She counted freight cars as we waited for trains at crossings; the peas in her dish; petals of flowers; people in stores.

She copied our every act and word; but she would not learn her boundaries. I tried many ways to keep Joy from untouchable items, with no apparent success. A slap on the hand might stop her from touching the heater one day, but not the next. Several times she burned her hand, having learned nothing from previous experiences.

One day's events are still vivid in my memory, nearly thirty-one years later. We put an expensive ornamental ashtray on the coffee table—a gift too pretty to store unseen. I told Joy she must not handle it. She reached for it. I said, "No. No." She eyed me slyly as she reached again. I slapped her hand. She screamed and then grinned and reached once more. This time I spanked her bottom. She howled angrily. I assumed the subject was closed until she grinned and reached for the tray, her eyes riveted on me. I snatched it from the table and put it in the cupboard out of Joy's reach, ignoring the advice in one of the baby books. That author obviously had never experienced a child like Joy!

Similar day-to-day incidents kept me busy—and edgy.

One morning I went to answer the telephone and noticed Joy ambling out of the room. Past experiences had taught me that long conversations were out of the question, and this call would be short. Before I could complete the call Joy returned, her hands dripping. I interrupted my friend's sentence and hung up the phone, wondering what Joy had done this time. She said nothing as I hurried her to the bathroom to wash her hands. I found my answer in the toilet.

Joy had put her sleepytime blanket in the stool. She looked up at me and grinned as I pulled the dripping thing from the toilet. She screamed in rage as I washed it in the tub and squeezed it viciously, venting my anger on it instead of Joy; and then hung it outside to dry. Her tantrum was violent and long, but the day was endless as I pondered why Joy had acted in such an inexplicable way.

Another afternoon's events left me in a similar quandary. Mild discipline and explanations had not kept Joy from playing in the water in the bathroom. The first time she stopped up the sink and turned on the faucet we had a near flood. I spanked her hands and told her she must never, never do it again. I took her downstairs to see where the water was ruining the ceiling of the apartment below. I asked if she understood and Joy nodded her head. Foolishly I believed her.

The very next day, as I was frosting a cake, Joy strutted into the kitchen to announce, "'You' made a mess, Mommy." I dropped the spatula and ran instinctively to the bathroom. An inch of water stood on the floor. Aghast, I spanked her bottom soundly and then yanked off her soggy shoes and sox and plunked her onto the sofa before mopping up the mess.

Scolding Joy did no good. Perhaps scolding myself

would have some effect, I thought as I wiped my eyes and blew my nose. "You goofed again, Jane. You're a total failure as a mother!" And then I prayed for guidance when I noticed Joy was no longer screaming. Instead she was watching me intently, with a big grin on her face. I knew the stopped drain was no accident.

It seemed Joy watched for occasions when I could not give her my total attention, and enjoyed seeing the messes she made and how I reacted. She repeatedly poured baby lotion, bath oil, perfume or hand lotion on the floor, furniture or herself. Cookies were for eating—sometimes. Other times she rubbed them into the carpet and then yelled at the top of her lungs as I scrubbed up the mess—or begged for another cookie.

It distressed me to find Joy sitting quietly on the floor, ripping her clothes apart. Why did she pull a snagged thread in a sock, reducing it to threads, or unravel a sweater from one tiny break in the yarn? Why did she pick the hems from her dresses and the elastic from her panties, one tedious stitch at a time? And why did she rip her sheets and blankets into strips if one minute hole appeared? Why? Why? Always the question. Never an answer.

Differences between her and the neighboring children haunted me, tormented me and challenged me. I could not pinpoint them. I was mired in generalities attempting to isolate specifics. She was a confirmed nonconformist. Her actions were not *always* different and her physical slowness was not too unusual, but she was somehow different. We took comfort in the knowledge that she obviously was bright and quick mentally and wondered if she might be a genius. Maybe she would require special education when she started to school. We had never heard of special education, as such, at that time.

Our many questions fit into three general categories: Joy's deviant behavior, regurgitation and physical slowness. The latest pediatrician told me I worried too much and to go about the business of mothering in a more relaxed manner. He suggested I forget about how little Joy walked. As to her small feet, he said, "She'll be the envy of all the other girls when she grows up."

The next specialist said we were at fault, that we encouraged laziness by carrying Joy every time she reached her hands for us to tote her. He intimated Joy was manipulating us. "Make her walk," was his order. He had no comment when I told him that we suspected Joy's feet hurt her and it was terribly hard to ignore her pleading eyes and reaching arms. Jerry and I promised each other to look away and force her to walk.

If she walked more, surely she would strengthen her legs; and she might lose her "baby stomach," which protruded and gave her stance a peculiar character, somewhat like the balancing posture of a pregnant woman in her ninth month. She also bent from the hips to pick things from the floor, almost as if she could not squat or bend her knees—though she could. She also walked in an odd, stiff-kneed fashion.

During a checkup one doctor paid more than the usual amount of attention to Joy's bulging middle. His casual question was like a bomb's explosion. "Has anyone ever suggested that Joy has had rickets?"

The room whirled. My mind raced to our last month's contribution to the overseas mission and the starved and neglected children on big posters and in magazines. Only they had rickets!

When I did not reply, he continued. "I'm somewhat perturbed over your little girl's flaring ribs and distended abdomen."

With that dizzying word, rickets, came a new fear. I had fed Joy a balanced diet and given her daily vitamin supplements all of her life. It seemed impossible to entertain the thought. His next words jerked me back to the examination room. "I may be all wrong, but that's what it looks like to me. Give her lots of Vitamin D." Then he added, more or less as an afterthought, "Better build up her muscles while you're at it. She's pretty flabby."

No argument there. But I wondered if he had any new ideas on how to *do* it. Memories of her unused kiddie car and other toys flashed across my mind. What had we not tried? I asked if her tiny feet and poor balance affected her walking. "Forget her feet. Buy the cheapest shoes you can find and let her run. Or let her go barefoot."

I knew that this pediatrician was the father of seven children. I considered him knowledgeable and authoritative. Other doctors' diagnoses had been ineffective. We would give his suggestion a try.

I bought a large supply of Vitamin D on the way home, and then checked our encyclopedia to learn more about rickets and corrective measures. Symptoms of the condition included premature birth and unusually rapid growth. My throat felt tight, my hands clammy. Joy was a full-term baby but she had more than doubled her birth height in her first two years. I read on. "Lack of muscle tone in limbs and abdomen. Slowness to sit, crawl and walk." Those characteristics also fit Joy.

"Slow eruption of teeth." No problem there. Then I crossed off the next signs of rickets, enlargement of the ends of the long bones and knobbed appearance of the ribs. If the bones were misshapen I did not know about it and her legs definitely were not bowed. Then I saw gastroenteritic disturbances listed as a complication associated with the affliction and my heart sank.

Maybe. Just maybe he was right, and maybe the increased vitamin dosages would counteract any damages already sustained. We would also give her extra milk and double her time in the sun. As for muscular development, a logical source of help seemed to be the pre-school nursery being formed by a group of neighbors. It was worth a try, whether or not Joy actually had had rickets.

At the group's first meeting the leader suggested I teach Joy to roller-skate. Several of the other women agreed that skates were marvelous for building muscles. Perhaps they knew more about it than I. I viewed the idea as a grabbing-at-straws, wild notion, but it was better than nothing.

Various problems were aired at the meeting. I listened intently when one mother mentioned her two boys' "bull-headedness." I might learn something from her! It was familiar ground. As the woman talked I began to consider the possibility that Joy was testing me. She, of course, might be bored with the steady and close contact of only me most of the time.

The pre-school sessions sounded like the solution to many of our problems. Then I glanced across the room where the youngsters were busy with several toys—all except Joy. She sat quietly on the sidelines by herself, watching the other children play, sucking her thumb and twisting her hair.

That settled it. We would buy those skates immediately! Jerry agreed to work with me although neither of us expected much success in teaching Joy to skate. And work at it, we did. We supported her, ran by her side, picked her up, doctored her scraped knees and elbows and kissed the bruises. No amount of help enabled Joy to skate alone. We still had a problem with no solution in evidence.

Perhaps another try with the kiddie car would work. We took it from its storage place in the garage, dusted it, and Jerry oiled the wheels. The next warm and sunny day I took Joy downstairs and led her to the shining vehicle. She studied it intently, and then I helped her climb onto the seat. She sat still and refused to put her feet on the pedals.

Several days and several attempts later Joy agreed to place her feet where they belonged, and I pulled the kiddie car to demonstrate what she should do. "Push this foot first, Honey, and let the other one ride around. One foot at a time!" Over and over this routine we went, but Joy could not coordinate her legs and ride unassisted. Then I ran behind and pushed her legs on the pedals. She tried, but pushed with both feet at the same time. (Later I learned this is typical of cerebral palsied children, but thank God I did not know it then.)

Joy tried and tried, but it was impossible to control those pedals. We were making little or no headway with her muscular development, but she was outside in the sun. It was a victory, to some extent, but it seemed more of a compromise.

After one afternoon's session with the kiddie car, Joy noticed the puppy next door. She shrieked delightedly at its antics until he found a hole in the fence and bounded out of his yard to play with her. She stood still, screaming in terror when he jumped up and nipped at her hand. She made no attempt to run, but seemed frozen to the spot. I grabbed her in my arms, and eventually calmed her after the pup scampered back to his side of the fence.

When quiet was restored I wondered why Joy had not tried to run away from the dog. Then panic took over completely. Joy had *never* run! Obviously she should have been running long ago. This was proof to me that something was definitely wrong with Joy's feet or legs. It might be rickets after all.

What amazes me, in thinking about that day now, is that both Jerry and I had become so accustomed to Joy's walking that we had not noticed her inability to run. We were advanced cases of shortsightedness!

We had overlooked many other things also. At three, Joy should have been able to climb up and down steps one foot at a time, I realized. We had fallen into a rut, noticing only her accomplishments. It finally dawned on us that Joy was neither lazy nor unmotivated. She was lethargic.

A clinical look was not possible, but we tried to assess Joy without emotion, excusing no peculiarities. We groped for an understanding of our child, acknowledging our ignorance of psychology and the criteria for determining normal behavior. I did double time on my knees, praying for God's help.

Typical of the inconsistencies and incongruities that ruled out flat statements as to what we could expect was her refusal to learn the changing use of the words "you" and "me" and "I." She stubbornly referred to herself as "you," and I was "me." The switching is confusing, I admit; but suddenly this mixup developed into a symptom.

I watched Joy even more closely, alert for more insight

into her complex nature; and life developed into a tight-rope circus act. Doubts nagged our decisions in even trivial matters as we searched for clues to the many contradictions of our beautiful little girl. If Joy knew her reasons for unusual actions, they were her secrets. They were as elusive as a mosquito in a darkened room.

She mimicked my actions and we bought miniature housekeeping tools, but they lay unused. Instead of drawing on her blackboard she demanded that I make the pictures. Instead of moving around, she wanted me to read to her or operate her record player. If the record ended and I was not handy to stop the player immediately, the loud rasping noise terrified her. She refused to touch it although she enjoyed the music it made. I soon developed a violent dislike for that item!

She had always loved music and we used it to calm her when she was upset or hurt. She began to cry every night at bedtime, so one of us sang lullabies or chanted familiar nursery rhymes; and when we sang "Jesus loves me," she joined in and never missed a word.

The books did not ban our standing by the bed to caress her or rub her back even though rocking chairs were taboo at that time. (I suspected that most of the authors of books on babies were childless!) When Jerry was home, he carried her from chair to table to picture to lamp, telling each a fond goodnight. The love he and Joy shared was beautiful to behold.

She reacted differently to Jerry than to me, probably because of his long absences at work. He did not believe our problems were as critical as I claimed and cautioned me against exaggerating and making molehills into mountains. Apparently her peculiarities were *my* problem, not *ours*; and I began calling Joy "my child." I snapped at Jerry's criticism and felt sorry for poor me. Our relationship suffered.

Life looked cheerier when Jerry was offered a cross-country transfer. We would miss living near the shore, but life in the Midwest had many benefits. We both hoped it would mean more time at home for him. Joy and Jerry needed each other, and I needed Jerry and the support his presence gave me in handling Joy.

We had high hopes as we packed and moved to the smaller city, temporarily diverted from worries about Joy's physical development and unusual mannerisms. We found a pleasant duplex and set up housekeeping.

Soon after we were resettled, however, the familiar doubts and fears resurfaced to dominate my waking hours. And instead of decreasing, Jerry's long hours and absences from home increased—sometimes for several weeks at a time when a tornado or damaging ice storm resulted in many insurance claims being filed over a widespread area. Jerry had to check out each one and process it for appropriate settlement.

Outings for just the two of us were rare, and limited to dinner and a movie or window-shopping. Our marriage would have benefited from more "dates," but it was simpler to stay home. I found it extremely difficult to locate a competent sitter or one who would come a second time. Then, too, we never knew what to expect on our return. We sometimes had a pleasant account of our bright and beautiful little girl, a peacefully sleeping child, a sick baby, or questions which I found embarrassing and we could not answer.

One woman told us that, quite frankly, she did not

understand Joy and would not come again to sit with her. I preferred her candid truthfulness to the vapid lies of others who assured me that Joy was a delight, but were consistently "busy" when I called again. Teenagers seemed puzzled by Joy. They played with her and were not analytical. Still, I recall one girl in particular.

As I counted out the money to pay her, she casually inquired, "Is your kid crazy?" My cheeks burned. No choice retort came. I hated myself for saying nothing, but what was there to say? "No"? It occurred to me that she had put into words a haunting fear which I could not admit, even to myself. Joy appeared to be above average in intelligence, but her actions were baffling.

If Joy actually did have superior intelligence, how could I cope with the situation? None of the experts' books contained chapters devoted to genius children. Nor did they spell out guidelines for parents of children of abnormal mentality.

The seeds of doubt sprouted and were nurtured by Joy's odd actions. As they grew, they spurred new analyses and it became clear that while Joy copied our adult speech she did not understand the words she used.

One incident stands out clearly in my memory. She stood before the full-length mirror, twisting and squirming as I pinned the hem in a new dress. "Mommy, *you* just *adore* this beautiful dress; but *you* don't like it. It isn't pretty." At the time I thought it was funny and I laughed at her confusion. She began laughing, too, and we hugged each other. Later I told Jerry, and the three of us laughed again. Then Joy repeated the sentence three times, word for word, laughing merrily each time as if it were a totally new thought. At the time we regarded it as cute and sweet and funny.

Joy's triple-talking caused day-to-day confusion. I recall one incident with mixed emotions. One Sunday afternoon she asked an ice cream vendor in the park for a cone, three times. He stood quietly, apparently wondering if she wanted three cones for the three of us. Perhaps his bewilderment stuck in my memory because of the important happening that day—an event which still evokes a gush of sentiment.

Joy gave me my first bouquet of dandelions. She picked each buttery yellow blossom, bending from the waist, and then strutted stiff-kneed toward me. She was proud of her gift, and I was pleased as punch. Then she noticed one dandelion which was different. It had gone to seed. When the ball of fluff disintegrated in her hand she studied her fingers, glanced at the ground, and began to cry. No explanation satisfied her. She begged Jerry to carry her, sobbing noisily. Soon she was sound asleep over his shoulder, and we headed home. Joy never picked another dandelion bouquet for me.

Similar bittersweet occurrences compounded our perplexity. New worries joined familiar fears, and pessimism overwhelmed optimism as questions multiplied. "Why" dominated the whole.

Her habit of repeating words or sentences was not a childlike practice to outgrow. She does it now. Regardless of an answer or comment, Joy still says the same things over and over again or poses the same question repeatedly. It does not bother us now that we have learned the habit's clinical term, "perseveration"; and that it is a characteristic of learning disabilities.

Life had triumphs and defeats then, and I teeter-tottered from pinnacles to potholes. Something was radically wrong, I suspected, but could not identify the problem. Fear became voracious; it gnawed at our complacency until we doubted our every act. The trial and error method had failed. I had tried, and I had erred so many times that I doubted any new approach would succeed. What motivated Joy yesterday bored her today. Tomorrow? Would it be better? I became overly watchful and skeptical, alert for problems. I put too much emphasis on insignificant happenings. Or did I? Did I expect too much of Joy? Or not enough? Did I stress trivial victories? I didn't know; for in the constant state of turmoil, I was unsure of everything.

After one particularly worrisome day of seeking clues and watching for unusual traits, I begged Jerry to move from the duplex. If we lived in a house in another neighborhood there might be playmates available for Joy, and she could copy their actions instead of mine. She would learn how to be a little girl. He agreed, and so we moved.

We transferred our church membership, happy to have a new set of Sunday school nursery attendants. The quizzical looks of former workers could be forgotten. We had a new slate—all new and better! Both Jerry and I assumed volunteer teaching assignments, but not in Joy's department. I needed the short Sunday respites!

Our new neighborhood teemed with children of all ages. We invited the youngsters to play, inside and out. I baked cookies and Jerry built a sandbox. The children came and played and ate the cookies and drank the cold pop—and Joy sat on the edge of the circle watching them. When they ran and played with her ball she watched them from the porch steps.

The light in her unusual eyes flamed high with interest for brief periods, then it wavered and went out. She seemed to be looking far away as she sat and picked at her fingernails, or twisted her hair while sucking her other thumb. Joy appeared to be totally unaware of the other boys and girls. Yet that night she repeated almost verbatim their conversation as they gobbled my oatmeal delights.

Then, one beautiful, wonderful, glorious day the whole future brightened. God had heard my prayers! Joy ran! She ran all the way from her sandbox to the back porch—about fifteen feet. She *ran*! At three and a half, Joy ran! God could not have missed hearing my thanks.

chapter **3**

Months stumbled into years and Joy graduated to a youth bed. She missed the crib and its pastel decoration of butterflies and frolicking lambs. We hoped the new, more grownup bed would inspire more mature behavior and she would outgrow both her bedwetting and compulsive vomiting. We also hoped the crib would have a new occupant.

Doting grandparents scoffed at any mention of oddities in Joy's actions and pressed for an early entry into school. Perhaps they saw the situation more objectively on frequent visits. Maybe, they suggested, she was intellectually superior and bored with a steady diet of only me for companionship.

Because the law was inflexible on the age factor, we enrolled Joy in a nearby nursery school. Two teachers shared the responsibilities, and I was secretly relieved to have three free hours daily.

Our hopes of any marked improvement did not last long. The two young women were hesitant at first, but conferences soon became commonplace occurrences as they and I joined forces to seek ways to handle unusual situations.

They said Joy did not participate in the games, she could not or would not finish projects, but she was a quick learner of songs and rhymes. I nodded. Then they mentioned Joy's destructive bent, but I was unable to give them her reason for tearing her clothes or possessions. They asked why Joy could not put on her own wraps; and I told them she took a long time to do so at home, but that she did dress herself. Of course, there were no other children to afford distractions at home to slow her actions.

The teachers assured me that Joy was a precious child and that they wanted very much to be of help to her. They asked for suggestions on ways to motivate her. It struck me as ludicrous. My experience was limited to one little girl, but they were in the business of handling children of all types. I was shocked to think that maybe they had never encountered a comparable child!

The older teacher commented that while it really was not her business and she hoped her suggestion would not offend me, she thought another child might take care of some of Joy's problems. I nodded. I realized, better than she, that Joy was a "lonely only." But to have a child for that purpose only would not be right. I did not mention that I had already lost two babies—one early the past summer. We had hoped for four but would count ourselves lucky to have two. The conference had not helped me.

The books and articles on mental illness which I read in secret had clued me into watching Joy for unusual gestures and mannerisms and actions. None of the things in the books fit her exactly. Was Joy schizophrenic? Was she emotionally disturbed? Was it a personality conflict between us? Was I merely dubbing a technical term to cover it or was I just a dumb, dumb woman?

Clinical terms became familiar as I furtively read more books and magazine articles on all phases of abnormal behavior in children. I became more and more frightened and bewildered. Based on what I read, it seemed obvious Joy was not mentally retarded. Our "perfect" little girl was in some way flawed. She did many obnoxious things that we had vowed our child would never do.

When I read the definition of paranoia I flinched. I would work at not blaming others for my problems, especially those sticklers not founded in concrete reality. What was real and what was unreal? I pondered. Did the neighbors and congregation pay excessive attention to us and were they talking about us? Was it a persecution complex on my part? What would happen to Jerry and Joy if I had to have therapy at some mental clinic?

Jerry was most annoyed when I told him of my fears. The conversation increased our daily tensions. Our relationship was sometimes precarious. I know now that Jerry was under considerable pressure with his new job, and in making ends meet financially. The everyday hassles of the workaday world overshadowed Joy's problems, which he did not see as often as I. How glad I am that he understands now and that he was more levelheaded than I then. Possibly God arranged things that way; for if Jerry had not kept an even keel, I know I could not have survived.

Everything was chaotic. Even shopping for groceries or in department stores was a nightmare. Joy continued to wander away from my side and many times she sat on the floor and screamed that her mommy had left her, much to my embarrassment. At least her loud crying helped in locating her.

Searching for ways to cope, we stumbled along blindly. If we could discover something that really mattered to her, life would be simpler; but few toys had much impact on her. She did love to splash in water and listen to music. We kept the record player handy because of music's calming effect. Joy responded to the tempo, keeping time with her feet and hands. And she sang and played with her dolls and in her sandbox, sat on our porch to watch other children at play, sat on our laps for storytime, and thoroughly enjoyed a bubble-filled tub or her plastic pool in the summer months.

We invited other children to play with her, and Joy appeared eager to have the companionship; however, they came less frequently as time passed and rarely invited her to their homes. When they came, she sat by herself picking at her fingers or toes, pulling a thread from her clothes, or twisting her hair while they grabbed the newest and best toys. Her principal social contacts were in the Sunday school class, one hour a week, with a captive group of companions.

The summer after Joy turned five we enrolled her in a dancing class, for three reasons: she would have companions, the music might encourage activity, and the exercises would strengthen her legs.

The first couple of weeks Joy anticipated the sessions and delighted in showing her leotard and shoes to the neighborhood children. Jerry and I exulted. We had finally done something right!

Our back-patting did not last long. Doubts resurfaced when the teacher remarked that Joy's stance was odd and that her coordination was "not quite right." Joy was always a beat or so behind the music and her reactions

were not properly timed. We agreed but had no suggestion for a remedy. It was not crucial that Joy be a
ballerina; and since she apparently found pleasure in the
class, we continued the instruction.

On another occasion, her teacher mentioned Joy's
dawdling in the dressing room after class. She sat and
watched the next group dress, picking at herself or her
clothes, or digging at a scab on her knees or elbows from
one of her frequent tumbles.

Before long the teacher suggested we not waste the
money on more dancing lessons. We had noticed no improvement in coordination, muscle tone or actions. Jerry
thought maybe she would do better on a backyard gym
set. Dancing lessons were terminated. Joy seemed not to
mind withdrawing from the class.

The box of pieces, poles, nuts, bolts and instructions
arrived on perhaps the hottest day of the year. Jerry
labored all one Saturday afternoon fitting the various
pieces together. At long last the set was assembled—
sturdy and safe. We stood back to admire the result of his
efforts, sweating in the mugginess of a midwestern late
August day. Joy could scarcely wait to give it a try.

She squealed with delight as we pushed the swing,
enjoying the cooling breezes and the newness of the
equipment. When it slowed to a stop, she asked us to push
it again, refusing to exert any effort herself. We demon-
strated how to use her feet and legs and back, but Joy sat
motionless. She would not use her legs and feet to push
the pole swing or climb the slippery slide. Repeated
efforts to teach her how to work the various parts were
wasted. If we didn't do the physical work for her, she
wanted no part of anything.

Jerry looked my way, confused by Joy's actions. When she left the gym set and ambled over to the sandbox I avoided Jerry's disappointed look. We trudged into the house to reread the books for ideas on muscular development, but we had already tried them all.

"Janey. Do you think it's her feet?" I could not answer; but when he suggested we consult an orthopedist instead of the pediatrician, I said it sounded logical. We scanned the yellow pages and made an appointment with a nearby specialist.

Joy seemed not to mind the examination of her feet but she hated the unrelenting stiffness of the corrective shoes he prescribed. Neither they nor the increased walking and foot exercises lessened her falls, which had already caused a broken elbow and two arm fractures. Joy continued to ask that we carry her. Her tiny feet surely hampered her balance and coordination, but no one had yet indicated a deformity of any kind. That came later when Joy was thirteen!

She removed the shoes as soon as possible and strutted in her peculiar fashion, barefooted, until school resumed. Joy was anxious to be on her way when the long-awaited first day in school arrived. She was alert, eager and animated, with her eyes shining brightly. She even stood still as I brushed and then braided her auburn hair into neat pigtails, which glistened like burnished bronze. Then she fidgeted as I tied satin ribbons to the braids. Joy commented that the ribbons and her new dress matched perfectly. She admired herself in the mirror and then posed while Jerry took a whole roll of color photographs to swell our bulging album. The momentous occasion was duly recorded.

Our hopes were alpine-high as she marched off to school with two neighbor children, happy to be included in the block-and-a-half walk. Jerry reached for my hand as the threesome strolled schoolward. "She's as beautiful as the day she was born." Jerry's words boosted my morale, but I wondered if he was as frightened as I and was telling himself that everything would really be all right. Only time would tell if kindergarten would be different from nursery school or dancing lessons.

Time did tell.

At noon, when it was time for Joy to return from school, I waited on the porch to greet her. Down the street she came, ambling along, alone. She carried her shoes, walking in her stockings. Her hair hung limp and bedraggled. One ribbon was lost and the other was chewed and frayed into a soggy mess. The hem of her new dress sagged between double knots which had defied her fingers. And Joy smelled of sour spit-up milk.

Shock kept me speechless, but Joy was animated as she described her introduction to regular school. Her appearance did not seem of any consequence as she bubbled and chattered like a string of popping firecrackers. She loved school! She adored her teacher! Then she sang a new song and recited a new jingle. Joy told me there were twenty-six in her room—eleven boys and fifteen girls. Then she told me of the milk and cookies the children had been served as a treat before rest time.

That first day in school was a milepost for Joy. She began calling me "Mother," and never again used "Mommy" except when she was sick or hurt.

Her account of the class activities interested me greatly. But what had the teacher thought of Joy? How did the other children react to her? How soon could I visit the class and see its operation? I must be careful not to put ideas of oddities into the teacher's mind. Had she seen the hair ribbons and dress hem? It seemed that school was no different from home. Of course, three short hours were not a true test and the next day or week might be better.

Truthfully, it came as no surprise when the teacher telephoned me in less than a week. She wanted to discuss a "couple of points before they develop into problems."

I dragged myself to the conference the next afternoon and found only the familiar questions—ones to which I had not yet found answers. "What are Joy's interests? How do you cope with her destructive tendencies? Is she allergic to milk? Why is she so sleepy much of the time? How do you motivate her?"

Now what do I do? Feign ignorance or be frank and candid? I realized stalling or hedging would help nothing and shivered involuntarily on the sultry day. Then I admitted I had no ideas to offer or suggestions to make. I could not take my fears from their hiding place and ask questions which might worsen the situation.

The teacher's problems were familiar, but fewer than mine; my mending basket, filled to overflowing most of the time, was *my* problem, not hers; and she had Joy only fifteen hours a week. Those nine hundred minutes couldn't compare with the fourteen hundred and forty I faced each day that school was not in session. Her hundred and eighty minutes a day were a breeze! And the sixty or so spent at the conference were wasted. Neither of us learned anything new, and finally I bade her goodbye and left the school.

Hurrying homeward, I reviewed the conversation—

the teacher's remarks and questions, to which I had listened intently. She had not mentioned any dread conditions, and she did say that Joy was aptly named—most of the time. She had not used any of the clinical terms which I dared not utter. Neither did she suggest brain damage; however, "minimal brain dysfunction" was a rarely used term at that time—and no one had yet mentioned it to me.

We placed a great deal of hope in the future, expecting time to provide curative powers. Surely first grade would do what kindergarten had not done, especially if Joy actually was a genius child and bored with unchallenging situations. The structured learning programs might produce marked improvement in her development.

Her first week as a first grader boosted our hopes. Again, she said she loved school and her teacher. Reading, spelling and arithmetic brought her a steady array of successes. Joy also made a few friends in addition to the four younger children in our neighborhood. Two little girls became her fast friends. Joy followed their lead, waiting and following their actions, speech, and their mannerisms. After-school playtime extended into overnight visits and Joy glowed.

She had a captive play group at Sunday school and then fidgeted while sitting with us for church services. She scribbled on the programs, practicing the alphabet and adding and subtracting the problems I wrote for her, or drawing "people" and "animals." She stood with us to sing the hymns and quickly memorized the more familiar verses and devotionals. The sitting-standing breaks in the service kept her from becoming too restless. But toward the end of a sermon her actions became disruptive and

made it difficult to listen to the minister. She enjoyed the
handshaking and socializing that followed the benediction,
acting like an adult rather than a child.

One major victory outranked most successes. The general practitioner we contacted for an emergency illness
prescribed a "simple medication" which controlled Joy's
regurgitation—at age six. He did not name it and I did
not think to ask what it was. Now we knew that Joy's
spitting up was not caused by a spastic stomach, an
allergy, or a need for attention. He said it was nothing to
be alarmed about, and assigned it no particular term. The
medicine was something to shout about!

Now we could take Joy to visit friends confidently and
could eat in restaurants. We could go for outings without
carrying a complete change of clothing, and the laundry
load would be much lighter. The most significant benefit
surprised us, for Joy had never evidenced much shame in
her frequent vomiting and had never complained. I wept
when she said, in a matter-of-fact way, "Now the kids
won't tell me to stay away from them because I stink."

Joy must have suffered greatly, but she carried the
hurt deep within herself. It was typical of her, I realize
now. She rarely complained about anything, although she
cried to show her hurt or anger, a habit which exists even
today. But she rarely verbalized her feelings.

Many times throughout her life I have been startled
when I heard her crying long after I assumed she was
sound asleep. A few times she confided in me, and efforts
to soothe her or comfort her eventually stopped her sobbing and she fell asleep. On other occasions, only she
knew the problem. Once she said that her teacher had
asked some questions that she could not answer, but she

refused to say what those questions concerned, regardless of my probing.

Inability to answer a question seemed to embarrass Joy, who inherited some of her grandfather's perfectionist traits. She usually tore up her papers and began anew rather than erase an incorrect answer. She seemed unable to comprehend that this consumed much time and was the reason she finished few assignments.

We played a game of school where I was the pupil and Joy was the teacher. I corrected the errors and then, to demonstrate the superiority of using an eraser, tore the original paper to shreds and reworked the problem. Joy timed the procedures and noted the time difference. Our game had no effect on her approach to real school lessons, however.

Jerry and I "hit the heavens" when Joy brought home a series of perfect test papers in spelling and arithmetic. True, they were short, but so very, very encouraging! Written comments from her teacher, and gold stars pasted to the tests made those papers worth framing. I bragged to anyone who would listen when the teacher told me that Joy helped the slower readers, acting as her aide!

I did not brag about less happy matters. For instance, making decisions of any kind was difficult for her. Indecision once caused a broken arm. She waited in line to climb to the top of the playground slide. Then, at the top, she seemed unsure of what to do. She may have been afraid. While she stood there the other youngsters waited impatiently. The girl behind finally gave Joy a good push and down she went to the ground. Both lower right arm bones were broken.

The cast was well autographed, and its nuisance value

diminished quickly. Not only was it an attention-getter, it brought to light Joy's ambidexterity. Her left hand assumed a new role.

Joy's indecisiveness also caused several unpleasant scenes at home before school. When she first started I offered her a choice of dresses. After a lengthy deliberation she would select one; but once dressed, she would cry and scream that she really wanted the other. Joy seemed unable to think for herself and abide by any decision. The only way to cope with this situation was to offer no alternative.

Her clothing held much importance in our lives. Many times Joy returned from school with a sash untied and dragging on the ground or lost if it had not been firmly attached. Sashes were of less consequence, however, than the damage she did to the dresses, socks and underwear. She ripped her clothes into strips, picked out the seams and hems, and left pockets dangling or completely removed. My stock question, "Why did you do it, Joy?" netted a shrug. A thread was loose so she pulled it. That was sufficient reason for Joy, who seemed unperturbed by my irritation. Why? Why? The word dominated my days.

"Why did God do this to me?" And "Why does God allow this situation to continue?" were a couple of the questions which eddied in my mind. Then I listened intently to one particular Sunday's sermon as the minister discussed self-pity and the motive people have for blaming God for unpleasant situations which they cannot control or correct. "Discover God's love and begin anew. Be careful that the present does not 'drive you crazy,' for the past is prologue—a shelter allowing us to be insulated from the problems of today."

His words led to more self-analysis. The sermon seemed meant for me, especially as the minister closed with the admonition to have courage to face each moment and forget the problems of the past. "God gives each person only the amount of trials and tribulations he can bear."

"Ha! He overestimated me!" I thought. Joy was busy raveling a new pair of socks instead of writing or drawing on the program. I was back at the dead end, "Why?"

The "pity-poor-me" days increased with my waistline. I was pregnant, and unlike my uneventful first pregnancy with Joy, problems arose and the months dragged. Miscarriage seemed possible, as had happened twice before, but eventually my condition stabilized.

Jerry and I were giddy with delight. Because we doubted our chances of having more babies, both of us hoped this child would be a boy. I was a little timid about handling a son, but Jerry scoffed at my fears and reassured me that boys are no different to rear than girls and that I would catch on. After all, he had learned about handling a little girl!

Joy was elated when we felt it was safe to tell her of the coming baby. But time had no meaning to her. She expected it to be born that day or surely the next. When the time drew near, we took her crib from the basement. She was certain the baby would be in it immediately and every day or so she wandered into the bedroom to check. She stood by the side of the crib, stroking the mattress and sucking her thumb. Her sweet, innocent look touched my heart. Then I realized with a start that she looked exactly as she had at age two. But Joy was seven years old! She asked no questions about how we knew she would have a brother or sister, nor did she seem to notice my increased girth.

Eventually Jonathan arrived, howling and demanding his share of my time. He was really special, I told Jerry; and then made a mental note to reserve that word, special, for other usage. I had heard it as another term for retarded children.

Joy had been a totally different child and there were few comparison points between my two. She had been a chronic sleepyhead, but Jonathan fought sleep. She was a baldy, but he needed a haircut. He was taller, heavier and darker. He was strong and extremely active, and it took both hands and an arm to diaper him. Bathing him was a daily workout which left me sopping wet. His mischievous eyes seemed to tell me he knew I was his slave, loving his energy and exulting in his masculinity. Joy had been feminine and dainty, but this child was all male!

Joy did not display any signs of jealousy. She loved to hold her brother and play with him, under our close supervision of course. (I well remember how she mistreated her dolls.) When he was a bit older, she sometimes helped spoon vegetables or pudding into his hungry mouth until he decided to play, splashing strained spinach or beets in all directions. She didn't cry or slap him. She merely walked away. Now and then she wiped away the mess, but usually she waited for me to wash her face and change her clothes.

Joy also helped fold his diapers. Her folds were straight and the corners precise and sharp. One day I told her she was a perfectionist, and jerked back aghast when she screamed and cried, *"No!* I'm a *girl!"*

She calmed down fairly soon and seemed to understand

the meaning of the word and that being a perfectionist was no cause for shame.

Joy was a quick learner, but boredom and no challenge were possible causes of her lack of attention and day-dreaming. If Joy did, in fact, have superior intelligence, advancement into accelerated classes would help. We agreed to let Joy be placed in special groups for arith-metic, reading and spelling, with the understanding that more parent-teacher conferences would keep us abreast of developments. One teacher's comment stood out from the others: "Occasionally when I am talking with Joy I have an eerie feeling. She seems faraway and completely detached from reality."

I well knew the sensaton her teacher described, but until it was brought into the conference I had accepted it as a natural aspect of Joy's personality. It *was* eerie!

"Someone should wire me into Joy's wavelength! And someone ought to write a book on how to cope with a bored genius child," I told Jerry the evening after Joy's teacher called for another confab, soon after beginning the new experiment.

Joy was sailing along in the advanced classes, but her work in other subjects did not improve. Efforts to help Joy comprehend abstracts met with a "glazed, lost-in-space look." I nodded. "In sixteen years of teaching, I've never met any child like your Joy. I simply cannot moti-vate her, yet she is bright and sweet. I really love her, and *must* help her." Her feeling of inadequacy was mutual.

I dabbed at my eyes, unable to suggest anything which might interest Joy. "Music might help," her teacher said, hopefully but not convincingly.

True, she sometimes walked a bit faster if I played

peppy songs like "The Mexican Hat Dance," and "Old MacDonald Had a Farm" could change her mood from blue to rosy. It seemed logical that her infantile response to music could extend to her childhood and that a way might be devised to use it in classroom techniques. The teacher said she would work out something along that line.

Music may have been more motivational than any of us suspected. I don't know. One afternoon when Joy was later than usual in returning from school, I panicked. I gathered Jonathan up from his nap and set out to hunt for Joy. A couple of young stragglers said they had not seen Joy and the search continued to the schoolgrounds.

The playground was empty. The halls were deserted. Then, as I prowled from one room to another, I heard a one-finger rendition of "Jingle Bells." I quickened my pace, pushing the baby buggy as fast as possible. Near the end of the building I opened the door. There she was. Joy was blissfully unaware of anyone or anything except the piano. She sat on the bench, her feet dangling, picking out the tune.

Where had she learned to play the piano? Had she taught herself to play simple melodies? Was this the cause of her lingering after school so frequently?

I called to her, but she seemed not to hear. When I called a second time, she stopped playing, turned around, and casually said, "Hi, Mother."

Combined relief and anger surged through me, and I began to cry as I struggled to explain why she must come home right after school. Memories of the two times she had accepted rides with strangers sharpened my tongue. Joy stood quietly. She seemed to be deaf and a "curtain" dropped over her eyes. She was far off in her own private world.

She slipped off the bench and walked to the buggy, to talk with Jonathan and shake his rattle vigorously. We left the school, Joy strutting by my side with one hand on the carriage and the other in her hair. She struggled to remove the remaining rubber band and loosen the braid. "What are we going to have for dinner, Mother?" she asked, totally oblivious to my distress of only a few minutes previous.

At home I closed the bedroom door to ponder Joy's incongruities unseen. There must be a cause for Joy to continue lingering in the bathroom, laughing gleefully and holding long conversations with an imaginary friend. Why did she still wander from me in the market or department stores while I waited to pay for purchases and then scream in anger—or was it terror? That situation had been partially alleviated by my making identical mother-daughter outfits which aided in identification and reunion. But she continued her disappearance act regularly.

She also continued to dare me to spank her, eyeing me as she did something she knew was off limits and for which she had been punished before. Surely she understood—or did she? Our complex Joy was a paradox instead of a paragon, it seemed to me.

Joy's various oddities came up for review in search of clues. She regularly arrived home carrying her shoes but did not complain of pain. One day she walked home in the rain, carrying her boots and sobbing bitterly that her feet were wet and cold. Her reason for taking them off was that her feet squished when she took a step. When she fell into a trench which had been dug by the utility company just before a heavy rain, she made no attempt to get out by herself. Her howls summoned me; and it was I, not she, who wiped the sticky mud from her face and out of her eyes and mouth.

Answers and clues were not forthcoming and I decided that perhaps Jerry was right, and that I took everything too seriously. My inexperience as a mother was the cause of many problems. I vowed to relax and not look for trouble.

Those good intentions went for naught when the school nurse telephoned a few days after the trench incident. She wanted to talk about a situation but named no specific problem. We wondered if it was a routine call which she made to all parents and not about Joy's frequent falls and poor coordination. We tossed possibilities like bean bags. Then Jerry reminded me of my promise to relax. "Don't worry, Jane, until you have to. It's probably nothing at all."

A neighbor kept Jonathan while I conferred with the nurse, who offered me a cup of coffee while she shuffled through a stack of papers. "It's routine," I exulted. "Joy is only one of a lot of children whose parents are being called to school."

After a couple of minutes and the usual exchange of pleasantries the nurse casually asked if Joy had told us that her teacher had requested a hearing test be given Joy. She eyed me intently as I assimilated this news. How odd! Joy's hearing was superlative. "Joy has no problem along this line, according to the tests," she assured me.

Why did she bother to have me come to hear such

news? It didn't make sense to me. Then I learned her
reason for the conference. She took a deep breath and
asked, "Has any doctor ever suggested Joy might have a
brain tumor?"

I reeled. I wanted to scream, "No! No!" but just sat
there shaking my head—more to rule out such a possibility than to reply. Brain tumor? Surely she had not said
that. I had misunderstood her. "Brain tumor?"

She nodded. The two words terrified me, but I could
not cry. My mind raced as seven years of memories
flashed past. I jerked my mind back to the present as her
voice came into focus again.

She suspected a growth because of the faraway look in
Joy's eyes, inattention, clumsiness, peculiar actions, and
unusual growth patterns. I knew them all, remembering
the broken bones and casts, the "curtain" which cloaked
her eyes. Yes. A growth was a possibility. She may have
said more, but I did not hear it. She handed me a glass of
water and a box of tissues and asked if I would like an
aspirin.

Visions of Joy in a hospital, her shaved head swathed
in bandages, clouded my mind. I must have walked out of
the building and to the car and then driven home, but I
recall nothing now except placing a call to our doctor.

Luckily he was available and I laid the horrendous
possibility in his hands. He listened without interruption
as I repeated the conversation, and then he exploded.
"She ought to have her head examined! But bring Joy in
this afternoon. You don't need to make an appointment,
Jane. I'll look her over, but I don't think there's even a
remote possibility of any brain tumor. She is a little

slow—always has been, you know. And try to relax. If you want me to call a specialist, that's O.K. It won't hurt my feelings."

"You'd better recommend a head specialist for me while you're at it."

He laughed and assured me he would keep an eye on all of the family, both as a friend and an M.D. His calm reaction set my fears to temporary rest, and his thorough examination convinced him there was no growth of any kind on Joy's brain. The eye specialist who made a follow-up test confirmed our doctor's diagnosis.

Then I could cry, and it seemed the tears would never stop. To be one-hundred-percent positive there was no benign or malignant tumor, we next consulted a brain specialist for intensive testing. Joy seemed not to mind the poking and peering which proved no tumor existed; but her stiff and unusual walk and stance interested the latest doctor. He commented that he was convinced she had not suffered a bout of crippling polio, easily confused with viral infections; and suggested we have an orthopedist check Joy's feet again.

Polio had never before been suggested, but Joy had suffered several viral attacks. The next in the long and costly parade of specialists prescribed corrective shoes, which Joy promptly removed. We were back where we had started. We still had no idea what Joy's problem or problems was or were; but several dread conditions had been eliminated in the search.

chapter 4

W E STRUGGLED through the school year and then welcomed summer with its respite from conferences with teachers—and the nurse. Joy slept late but Jonathan was an early riser, which gave him and me several hours of time together. His independent nature and rapid physical development fascinated me and I reveled in being his mother.

Jonathan seemed unusually quick and was several months ahead of the timetables for development. He walked before he was six months old. He was agile, active and surefooted. It was apparent that our prayers had been answered and that the problems we had with Joy were not applicable to him.

The two played well together in the sandbox and they derived mutual pleasure from splashing in a big plastic backyard pool. Both had active imaginations, and it was pure pleasure to watch as they converted clouds into things. Puffy white "dogs" or an "old man with a long beard" became a "mouse" or a "rabbit" as clouds chased other clouds across the sky and then became wispy nothings. The animation was equal to the best of Disney!

I did not recognize the significance of one day's cloud

pictures until many years later. The children were playing
in the backyard while I hung the laundry to dry. Joy called
to me excitedly. "Mother! Look up in the sky!" She
pointed to a mass of puffy white clouds being broken by
the strong wind currents.

"There's God!"

The clouds did have a form that resembled a man. And
as we watched, a smaller man's shape appeared. "Is that
his Son, Jesus, Mother?"

I had no answer, marveling at her faith.

"They're both up there, watching over us, you know,
Jonathan," she said.

She was able to commune with God in her childlike
way and establish rapport unknown to adults. Never in all
of her thirty-four years has she doubted his love or
questioned his existence.

Joy read to her little brother, but she never made up a
story to tell him. One day I realized that she played this
way with her dolls and that she copied my speech patterns
instead of talking like her two friends, especially when she
was alone. I wondered if older playmates might help her
development. We continued to entertain her two friends
several days each week, and the three frequently spent
the night together. I vowed to widen her circle of friends
some way.

Picnics and holiday parties were good excuses to invite
children to play at our house, but I wondered how long we
could keep them coming. Little tots could be bribed with
cookies and treats and toys; and they seemed not to notice
that Joy sat on the side, watching as they played, and that
Jonathan was more involved than she. Joy was invited to
parties now and then, and she was overjoyed and helped

choose a gift and then wrap it. She would be so excited she could not sleep the night before such an occasion, and we soon decided to wait until the last minute to shop or mention the invitation. Also, she could not keep the gift a secret and always told the recipient what to expect.

Between parties and exchange visits with her two friends, Joy was a loner. Many times she sat on the edge of the sandbox and stared at the sky. Sunset's ever-changing colorama and the clouds entertained her for long periods of time, while Jonathan raced around the yard or played on the gym set.

Joy delighted in watching squirrels as they leaped and scampered from tree to tree or housetop, their tails fanning into graceful plumes. When they sat on their haunches, Joy would clap her hands in glee; and she mimicked them as they chewed on acorns, their mouths moving at lightning speed. When a cardinal perched on our feeder she became animated. Then, when he fed his mate a seed from his bill, Joy insisted they had kissed.

She loved the birds and squirrels and the cats and dogs that populated our neighborhood. The bright reds and blues of cardinals and jays excited her more than the robins' rusty vests, but she enjoyed watching them all. One spring, a pair of robins built a nest in the big old oak tree. We watched the daily progress and were rewarded by an occasional peek at the gaping bills of the babies when Mother Robin returned with their breakfast. A few days later a cat found the nest and we saw no more of the birds. Joy wept bitterly.

Despite her apparent fondness for animals, Joy panicked when any approached her. We settled for trips to the zoo and neighbors' pets which she enjoyed from the safety of a chain-link-fenced backyard. This was another in a series of contradictions.

Neighbors and our friends rarely mentioned their children; and I suspected Joy was the subject of discussion when several times their conversations stopped abruptly as I entered the room.

False pride kept my head high and my mouth closed, and I refused to ask their advice. There was little or no chance that they knew more than the professionals. I feared their labeling me paranoid. Surely the other mothers noticed that Joy waited briefly to note our reactions to jokes or stories, and then duplicated our actions. It was far from normal to laugh hysterically when someone was hurt and then cry and sob bitterly. No one called me when Joy meandered around the neighborhood and, if invited inside, made herself at home and stayed on and on for hours until I finally found her.

What did they think about Joy's parroting our speech and repeating expressions or questions four or five times? I wondered, too, at their reactions to her forgetting to go to after-school Brownie meetings and then crying in panic if I had taken advantage of the time to do errands and was not home to meet her.

Jerry brushed my concern aside. He was right in saying that their opinions really did not matter. They had no similar situations and no training to deal with our problems.

When left to her own devices, Joy preferred to sit and watch Jonathan as he daredeviled his way over and around a jungle gym. She also chose to play with the younger children in the "Y" pool, and paddled in the water with the youngsters.

"Let's try to keep her occupied outside, Janey. I noticed a group of kids with a jump rope the other day. We haven't bought her one of those, and it might strengthen her legs."

"Anything is worth a try. But don't expect miracles—at least for a day or two. I'll see if there is a place to buy one near here, tomorrow."

Joy struggled, but she could not control the rope and jump over it, so we bought a longer piece of rope and tied one end to the garage door handle. I shouted "Jump!" as the rope neared her shoulder to allow for her delayed timing. I turned and turned the rope before she would approach the jumping spot; and she did succeed in clearing it a couple of times. Her pleasure was beautiful to see, but the sessions left the two of us exhausted. My evening prayers included special thanks to God for Joy's new skill.

The near-success with the rope was heady and encouraged other exercises. Perhaps Joy could manage skates by now, and we cleaned and oiled them for a second attempt. It proved no better than the first, years ago; however, we considered ourselves lucky that she did not break any bones in her many tumbles.

The vacation months crept to a sweltering end. The school year loomed again with the daily ordeal of getting Joy out of bed instead of sleeping away most of the morning. The reward was the hours when I could enjoy Jonathan and give him my undivided attention.

A day or so after school began Joy begged for a bicycle because several of the neighbor children rode bikes to school and she felt left out. Memories of the kiddie car and tricycle did not inspire confidence, but we were willing to try anything which offered any shred of hope. We bought a bike with training wheels—and serious doubts.

After a couple of days, many falls, and scraped knees and elbows, Joy discarded the bicycle and returned to her record player, her puzzles and her dolls. She sat and cuddled one old beaten-up favorite, singing "Jingle Bells" as September's perspiration dripped down her neck and face.

Jonathan acquired the bike a short time later, at two-and-a-half; and Joy seemed not to care. She preferred her new occupation, playing school. Joy was the teacher and had a variety of "students." She tore sheets of paper from a tablet and passed them around to the imaginary class, issued instructions and then collected the test papers. The "students" who did not do well received lectures on their shortcomings and those who made perfect papers received written praise on their papers. Joy carefully stacked the blank sheets of paper on her desk after each school session.

Her new interest furnished an inkling of Joy's school experiences. Additional insight came in the familiar form of a consultation at school, with both her teacher and the principal. Previous meetings had been with only the one woman and the implications of a dual conference worried me as I headed for the school.

The principal, a charming woman with a gentle smile and a kiss of silver in her dark brown hair, greeted me and attempted to make me comfortable. She prefaced the conversation with compliments as to Joy's abilities in some subjects and added that Joy was a precious little girl. "She is not a problem child, Mrs. Jennings. No indeed! She is a child with a problem, however. I wish I knew what it is, but none of us does. She is deep. Sometimes I feel as if she is not 'with us,' but living within herself."

There was nothing I could add, and the teacher continued the conference. "Joy is far ahead of herself in many ways, and it is difficult—or more, impossible—to keep her interested for long periods of time. When she escapes, figuratively speaking, or is bored, I let her go to the office. Did you know she has taught herself to type?"

"No. She's never even mentioned a typewriter or anything about visiting the office." It struck me as odd that the women had called me to school just to tell me about Joy's typing or that she had a problem that had existed since kindergarten. Fears whirled and eddied as I waited, dreading whatever it was that needed such cushioning.

The principal leaned forward, and in her most gentle way said, "Mrs. Jennings, we both admit we cannot offer much help to your daughter. We have discussed it at length, and we feel the situation demands attention from a specialist in child psychiatry."

She paused. Her words exploded like a time-release grenade, pelting me with shrapnel. Still, her words really did not surprise me. I think I had expected them sooner or later.

"With your permission, we will make the necessary arrangements."

"Yes, of course, We realize she requires...." I could *not* say anything more. Perhaps a specialized test would reveal the source of our problems. My mind raced over Joy's mannerisms and behavior—so smart at times and yet so.... The word which fit her actions, "stupid," hurt too much to say it aloud. It was a relief to have an ultimatum take the situation out of our hands. There was no choice. I felt positive Jerry would agree to the new examination, distasteful though it was.

Neither of us was enlightened enough to think of the world of mental health without shame and embarrassment. It was foreign to us—off limits—beyond our knowledge. We never mentioned Joy's testing to any of our relatives or friends. I had to know, and asked the principal if the test and results would be on her permanent records. "Only if it affects her grade placement. It will, of course, be confidential."

More doubts came to mind. If the tests were not necessary and nothing was gained, would we have done Joy an irreparable harm? How would she feel about it? Was the problem ours and not hers? Could Joy ever forgive us if it was another mistake? And would God forgive us? "Don't let us make things worse for Joy," I prayed.

The principal outlined the nature of the tests and said she would let us know the time and place as soon as she could set up the examinations and interviews.

After lengthy deliberation, Jerry and I agreed to the total examination and would answer any and all questions. Even long-hidden secrets would be dug from their abysmal burial places. We would spread our accumulation of unpleasant experiences for strangers to sift and sort, hoping this last-ditch effort would benefit Joy. It might resolve our frequent and increasingly heated arguments over Joy's discipline and training, and we could avoid seeing a marriage counselor.

And so the examinations began. Several specialists ran tests on Joy and began memory-raking interviews with us. We stressed Joy's academic superiority and her affectionate nature, soft-pedaling her mercurial temperament as

long as possible. We eventually bared our mistakes and
our fears and our bleak days and black recollections for
impersonal clinical appraisal.

The doctor noted Joy's full-term birth weight and my
small weight gain, at the obstetrician's insistence. I relived that entire first pregnancy. A bout with the flu early
in my third month was the only complication—I hadn't
even had morning sickness. The doctor pressed for details
of medication I used during my pregnancy. Then he
quizzed me regarding the delivery, but there was little to
tell. The shot of anaesthetic had taken effect at noon, after
one wave of labor pains, and lasted until early the next
morning. It had also stopped labor and apparently had
been too strong, although no one ever told us the details. I
awakened when Jerry told me we had a perfect little girl.

Clinical probing raked up old and healed injuries and
illnesses, and I recalled one nearly forgotten item. Joy's
tongue had been slightly tied and was snipped free a day
or so after birth.

We told them of our mistakes, the dreary and the
bright times, our pride and embarrassments and fears,
and our disagreements, many of which were self-indict-
ments. But I did not reveal one ugly secret. I could never
admit to anyone that occasionally I doubted my love for
Joy and sometimes almost hated her. I prayed to God for
forgiveness and guidance, and detested myself more and
more. Not even Jerry must ever know. God knew, and I
knew.

The doctors took copious notes during the several days
of testing and interviews, but they made no comment.
They merely asked questions, pressing for details, especially concerning Joy's destructiveness.

It was difficult to tell strangers that Joy shredded both blankets and sheets as well as her clothing, deliberately ripped wallpaper from her room, filled partially used bottles of shampoo or perfume or hand lotion with water, scratched her name on the walls and furniture, and had even hacked a chunk out of the brick hearth with Jonathan's toy saw. The ordeal went on and on.

"Has Joy ever told you why she does these things?"

I shook my head. "She always says she doesn't know or that there was a hole or break there already."

The doctors said nothing and the quizzing continued. We told them of the vision and hearing tests conducted at school because of her unusual reactions. They wanted to know more about her "sightless" look and her "faraway" attitude, but Jerry and I found it impossible to furnish much enlightenment about Joy's strange mannerisms.

The seemingly interminable conferences finally ended and the four specialists agreed to pool their information before our next session.

The impersonal meeting the following week chilled me with its sterile atmosphere and clinical language. Jerry sat in a roomy upholstered chair and I perched on a straight wooden chair near the desk, anxiously awaiting the diagnosis and prognosis.

The oldest man appeared to be in charge. In a heavy accent indicative of European birth, he told us that Joy was "a little slow and has a numbers complex." I was impatient for him to get to the point and not tell us things we knew well. He talked at length about her memory and her aptitude for arithmetic, and we strained to understand his broken English. Jerry was impatient to know Joy's I.Q. rating, and asked the doctor.

"She's not as intelligent as you think." We had expected frankness and candor and were disappointed at his vague response. "Treat her gently," was his advice.

The doctors indicated the session was over. We were back at our starting point, having learned little. Were they as baffled as we?

Riding home in silence I mulled over the conversation and was surprised when Jerry said, "How gentle is gentle? I think they gave us a runaround, or maybe she stumped them, too." He, too, was rehearing the doctors' remarks.

"Do you think they'll give the school the same diagnosis they gave us?" I asked. He shrugged and I continued, "We need help as much or more than Joy does. Neither of us understands her or her problem."

"If they don't tell the school any more than they told us, we wasted our time and money on the tests," Jerry concluded with a wry grimace.

"They sure didn't waste words on us anyway, and it was hard to understand the few that one doctor did use. If he gave her the tests it's entirely possible Joy couldn't understand him either. But she got a big bang out of their puzzles and the doll family—one man, one woman, and three children."

So far as we could tell, the exhausting ordeal had done little, if any, good. We knew no more than before but vowed to work overtime at being gentle with Joy.

Advancement in Jerry's job involved another move and held hope for us as a family. Again we hoped he might not have to be on the road so much and could live at home during the week. But it also meant a fresh start with new neighbors, classmates, teachers and doctors who might have a different insight to Joy's personality or problem. The smaller town we moved to, however, would be safer for her. There were fewer possibilities of people preying on her innocent and trusting nature.

The relocation meant leaving her two friends, a fact we hated. We hoped both Jonathan and Joy would be included in the activities of the several children who lived near our new house. We had chosen the place with that in mind. Jonathan was such an outgoing little fellow, we had no doubts that he would make friends quickly. Not so Joy.

Most of the youngsters were in Jonathan's age group, but two ten-year-old girls lived on our block and others were near. Many of them came to watch our furniture being unloaded, and some stayed to play. Life in the new community began with a happy thrust.

I felt fortunate that Jonathan's needs could be more nearly met through a larger number of playmates. Watching Joy took so much of my time that I frequently had to neglect him. I thanked God for his abundant self-sufficiency. I could not stretch myself physically to cope with the needs of both. He had to fend for himself.

Some of the youngsters attended our church and the Sunday school class was not a group of total strangers. Joy was interested in counting the windows and pews and choir seats. The junior choir was a social outlet and a source of pleasure for her.

We bought an old upright piano and arranged for music lessons. Joy signed up for swimming lessons at the nearby municipal pool. She was busy and happier than we had seen her in a long time, apparently having adjusted to the new town without difficulty. She was sailing along as school began in the autumn.

Joy said little about her new school, but this was not unusual. She never had told us much after the excitement of the first few days of each year. Three weeks passed and I began to think our troubles might be past history. Then our high hopes plummeted. The teacher called me for a conference.

He posed the familiar questions and asked new ones, adding comments which were enlightening and discouraging. "Some of Joy's classmates make fun of her. They take advantage of her gullibility and swap her out of her nice new crayons and notebooks and other things." He seemed a bit embarrassed to mention Joy's slowness, but felt compelled to do so. "A couple of times I've had to discipline her and a couple of the other girls because she makes bets—impossible bets, on foot races. And she always pays off. Of course that is forbidden; and when I caught them taking her money, Joy told me all about it."

Now it was clear why she had been shaking her piggy bank before leaving for school the previous morning. I wondered what else I might learn from this man, my daughter's first male teacher.

It was possible we would learn the identity of her taunters, the ones who had inspired her to ask the meaning of the word, "moron." I had explained as best I could that a moron was a person who had problems in learning, which seemed to satisfy Joy. She did not reply when asked why she wanted to know; but when pressed for an answer, said that some kids called her "Joy Moron Jennings" and then laughed and laughed but she did not understand the joke. I winced, recalling the incident, and despised her unnamed classmates.

We thought her name, Joy Morgan Jennings, had a

musical quality, and preferred my maiden name to some more common middle name. I wondered if Joy understood my definition of the odious word; and later realized it was obvious that she did know, full well, what they had said and meant. She renamed herself. Now she became Joy Lynn Jennings and refused to acknowledge her true name.

The new teacher also told us that "rote memorization probably accounts for her arithmetic superiority, but she seems to understand only concrete problems—no abstractions." I nodded. "Mrs. Jennings, Joy is either a genius or she has a photographic memory. I'm not sure which it is, but personally I think it is her memory that keeps her in the top group. I've never had a student like Joy."

"Who has?" I was tempted to ask as my mind flew to her memory feats. Just the last Sunday she had won a Bible for memorizing the most Scripture passages. And we never needed to consult a phone book or check an address listing if Joy had seen or heard the numbers.

"She waits to copy the reactions of the others many times, which indicates to me that she is unsure of the word meanings." This was familiar and I nodded again. "She reads well, but I doubt she comprehends the larger percentage of the words themselves."

His words rang true. There was nothing to add, although he seemed to expect an answer. He also seemed reluctant to go on, but took a deep breath and looked at me intently. "Personally, I feel she has 'book sense' but no common sense, Mrs. Jennings."

He recommended a clinical examination to determine Joy's status. The cycle was familiar. Tests and interviews, doubts and fears, more tests and more interviews. Those

were the positives. But how about the answers? Would
the teacher understand if I told him that we had already
been subjected to one exhaustive series of psychiatric
testing and that no one had diagnosed Joy's problems. It
seemed doubtful that there was much to be gained from
another; however, a new opinion might be worthwhile.
Again, it could be merely another dead-end ordeal to
endure. Such sessions in the small town atmosphere might
lead to embarrassment for Joy and us.

His words struck home as I left the teacher's office,
walked down the stairs and outside. His evaluation was on
target. It sounded plausible that Joy had memorized the
appearance of various words in her books and then copied
our reactions and words. She rarely ever asked the meaning of any word, and I wondered if she feared ridicule by
exposing her ignorance of some definition. Or had Joy
learned to read too early as I held her, reading and then
rereading the simple books? The conference had one thing
in common with all previous meetings with school people.
Questions. Questions, but no answers.

Why did Joy apparently not mind when younger children teased her? She ignored their chants: "Joy is a dumb
dumb. Joy is a dummy dumb." I minded! I hated those
children! And I winced when Joy told me some kids at
school had called her a bird brain after we tacked a sign to
our house, naming it "Jay's Nest." We had thought it was
a clever usage of our initials—every one of us was J.J.—
but she did not seem to realize they were making fun of
her. I was positive also that Joy did not understand the
words she casually repeated and that the profanities and
obscenities meant nothing to her. She laughed hilariously.
Nor had she understood why she was being punished for

uttering the foul words.

Nearing home I recalled the remark about Joy's arithmetic capabilities and an incident which occurred while she was recuperating from chicken pox, during the third grade. I attempted to tutor her. We were working on an assignment and it astonished me when she registered a total blank when asked how many pencils she could buy for fifty cents if they were priced three for a dime. When I rephrased the question in concrete form, "What is three pencils times five dimes?" she replied instantaneously, "Fifteen." Then she could not estimate the room's height when compared to her own.

It came as a jolt, and I stopped in the middle of the block. Her memory was an enemy—not an ally!

chapter 5

DAYS AND WEEKS became a blur. I remember one bright October day. Brilliant fall foliage brightened the horizon as dropping temperatures forecast red-nose-and-pink-cheek weather. Joy brought armloads of fallen maple leaves from a nearby park. When I commented on their redness, she corrected me. "They're burnt sienna, Mother." She had noticed that particular hue so identified on a crayon wrapper.

Many such incidents kept our hopes for the future high. Yet we knew we were hiding our heads in the sand, and we feared the foundations of our life were not secure. Perhaps her teacher's analysis was wrong; but if he was right, it seemed possible that her book sense might make up for her so-called lack of common sense.

Joy's inborn sense of music and memory blended to fascinate us even more. When she practiced her piano lesson, no one could force her to look at the printed music. She knew it without reading the notes.

Music continued to play an important role in Joy's life, and she used the piano to express emotion. When she was happy she sat and played for long periods of time. When angry, she pounded the keys; and music became a barometer of her moods.

Musical programs on TV held her attention as few other things could. Animated cartoons also gave her much pleasure, and she and Jonathan spent Saturday mornings watching them. Her large size accentuated the difference in their ages. It was all too noticeable when she insisted on joining him and his friends at play.

Several times I overheard the little boys and girls; and their remarks stung. I hoped Joy missed the ridicule, even though Jonathan did not. It hurt to see him embarrassed and attempting to shield her. He was too little to bear such a burden.

The neighbors undoubtedly noticed our peculiar situation; but Jerry suggested it was only my imagination that they discussed us among themselves. Our heated arguments settled nothing, and they became more frequent as the months muddled along and Christmas neared.

One day Joy left the group of little tots and came into the house crying. She refused to discuss the trouble, but later she said that one boy had told her and Jonathan there was no Santa Claus. Jerry and I had hoped to keep the myth alive at least for one more Christmas, and I was annoyed at the showoff know-it-all who had enlightened Jonathan. Then, with a shock, I realized Joy—not Jonathan—was affected! And last Easter she had been most upset when she caught us hiding the colored eggs. Could it be that she still believed that fable also? I promised to stop calling her our "Easter bunny!"

Joy definitely needed more companionship with children her own age. In desperation we decided that a party might help—it had worked before. This time it was different. Only about half of those invited came.

While making a guest list I had recalled that after the

newness of their acquaintance, other girls her age came to our house or invited Joy to theirs less and less often. Now and then a girl did accept, but the many differences in their actions and Joy's became more and more noticeable and worrisome.

Other girls whispered and giggled about boys, and I wondered how much Joy understood of my birds-and-bees discussion. She was not a child anymore, but she seemed and acted like one. She was on the threshold of adolescence, and the thought terrified me. Joy was trusting and vulnerable. She would be easy prey for anyone who might abuse her. New fears joined old and became permanent members of our family.

My prayers grew longer and more frequent. "Please, dear God, don't let her be hurt anymore. She's been hurt badly so many times already. Spare her. And show me what to do for her. Please!"

My need for God's help was urgent. I panicked each time Joy was a few minutes late returning from school. The experts had advised us to make her become independent and self-reliant and told us that if we expected too little she would produce less than she should or could. We must help her achieve her full potential by doing less for her.

Forcing myself to let her walk to and from school was a daily lesson in self-discipline. I abandoned the effort when I learned she was tardy quite frequently because of stopping to watch a cat or a squirrel or to visit with a neighbor.

Our problems should have been solved, but Joy took to dawdling instead of coming to the car promptly after classes. Five-year-old Jonathan was assigned to wait in the car while I searched for her. Several times we finally gave up and drove home, watching every side street along the way in hopes of catching sight of her with some other girls.

Another problem was the several exits from which she might leave. Frequently other people would offer her a ride, totally unaware that Joy was supposed to come out one specific door to meet me. Once at home, Joy would either sit shivering on the porch, crying because I was not there, or wander aimlessly around until someone invited her inside. "They invited me," was her stock reply when asked why she had not come to the car where she knew we were waiting, or why she had wandered off and not waited at home. All explanations were wasted efforts.

Winter's snow and chill winds helped keep Joy from walking around town, but spring's freedom brought new worries. When I was out of hearing or busy with some chore, she would frequently disappear. She roamed the neighborhood visiting and watching the neighbor's television. She stayed put until one of us found her. Fear lived with us and grew incessantly.

At night I relived my daytime worries. Would we ever find peace and happiness? Would Joy ever act her age? And how about neglected Jonathan?

Joy became even more a loner when Jonathan's friends refused to play at our house when she was present. She watched cartoons and juvenile programs. If sad scenes flashed across the set, she cried. And she first laughed and then cried when some actor was hurt or when one of her classmates or one of us was injured some way. She often sat quietly in her room working jigsaw puzzles or playing school by herself.

As the school year neared report card time, real people and classmates and her dolls lost their appeal for her. She preferred the company of imaginary playmates. One lived with us, ate with us, shared Joy's secrets, and was her constant companion. I wondered why "she" had no name. If "she" did, Joy never mentioned it or addressed her by it. She was "She." Joy spent considerable time locked in the bathroom, laughing and chattering animatedly with her invisible friend.

Her work in school began to slip, and she hid her report card from us. Eventually she handed it to me, tears streaming down her cheeks. I would work harder to keep her abreast of the class, I told Jerry that night. She obviously was ashamed of her poor record and needed tutoring of some sort. When she forgot or deliberately refused to bring home her books or assignments, we bought an extra set of texts to keep at home; but nothing succeeded.

"Be gentle. She's naturally slow," the psychiatrist had advised. He also said to be calm. It wasn't easy, as we spun on a merriless merry-go-round.

Joy was nearing thirteen, chronologically. Her body was changing but her behavior patterns remained static. Names and initials of "boyfriends" now appeared on her furniture, the walls, her books, on her purse, and in her conversation with "She." The only item she spared was her Bible. She tore pages from all other books and scribbled words or drew crude pictures on their covers. She was fascinated with her adolescent body and asked for a bra. She talked of girdles and formals and nylons, and smeared lipstick on her mouth, the house and our possessions as well as hers.

One day Joy announced she had a date. It sounded incredible and I pressed her for details. "I asked him to go to the dance," she said. She admitted he had not replied, but insisted that she had a date because she had invited him. That was that!

What way was there to make her understand? I was tempted to call the boy's mother and learn more. Perhaps it was false pride, but I yearned for the anonymity of the big city.

When the evening came, Joy primped like all teenage girls. No arrangements had been made for transportation to the party so Jerry drove her to the auditorium and then went inside with her. He stayed as a chaperone, danced with Joy a couple of times, and then they came home. She went upstairs and closed the bathroom door. Soon we heard her talking and laughing with her "friend." Much later she went to her room and prepared for bed.

Jerry broke the silence by asking, "What can we do about her interest in boys? It could get her in a heap of trouble. I felt so sorry for her at that party when nobody paid her the least bit of attention. She drank three cups of punch and ate about half a dozen cookies. Teachers and the other kids looked away when I danced with her. Her 'date' was there with a group of fellows, but nobody even said 'hello' to her."

"I don't have any idea what to do, Jerry. We can't import or bribe kids this age to keep her company the way we did when she was a little girl. I feel so sorry for her. She's so lonesome and vulnerable. Frankly, I'm scared to death of what could happen to her."

We headed for our room and as I walked past Joy's bedroom I heard her muffled sobs. She was wide awake in the dark. I hurried to her bed and she reached her arms to me. She pulled me and hugged me close.

"Honey. Sweetheart. Joy, darling. What's the matter?" Her sobs increased. "Don't cry. Tell me all about it," I urged. She continued crying heartbrokenly as I rubbed her back and patted her arms, hugging her tightly.

"Why don't the kids like me, Mommy?"

Mommy? Had she called me Mommy? She may or may not have believed me but I told her, "They do like you, Sweetheart. Of course they like you." I knew it was a lie. They did not like her. Very few children had ever liked her. Her first grade teacher had told me that Joy wanted to have friends but she did not know how. Yes, I lied then and I would lie again. Her hurt was great. She had called me Mommy.

When I was certain Joy had fallen asleep, Jerry and I discussed the recommendation made by her teacher over two years previously. It had not seemed right then, but things had changed. Now the clinical psychologist might produce better results than had the battery of specialists who had examined Joy earlier.

Before we took this step, however, we would work at the housework and keep-Joy-busy effort. More testing would be only a last resort.

Our intentions were good, but we had not consulted Joy. She reacted as before, doing things in her own way and at her own speed, if and when she felt like it. Sometimes both of us were totally exhausted from the effort of making her sweep the bedroom and dust her furniture, vacuum the living room or dry the dishes.

She resented the new restrictions on her activities and lashed out at me as if she hated the very sight of me. She always had had a vicious temper when angered, although most of the time she was docile and lethargic. Now she swore and used gutter language if we crossed swords. Her threats of bodily harm were frequent although I doubt she intended to follow through. Housework was not the solution.

Her behavior and words embarrassed Jonathan and he began avoiding family outings. He preferred to stay home alone or to play with a friend while Joy and I shopped or did errands. I knew he was not old enough to leave home, but I also knew how he felt inside. I, too, found Joy a source of embarrassment at times and hoped no one guessed my secret. I was saddled with a difficult choice and wished for the wisdom of Solomon. It may have been wrong but I relied on Jonathan's self-reliance and prayed a lot.

I fear I was partial to Jonathan many times, especially on bad days when it was not easy to love Joy. I could not understand her and I could not cope with her.

I recall one day in particular. It had been unusually pleasant and uneventful. After lunch I discovered that Joy had dumped out most of a box of detergent and there was not enough to do a load of laundry. Asking her why she had done it—and I was positive that she had emptied the box—would be a waste of time. I did, however, scold her and tell her not to repeat it.

The car would not start and she volunteered to walk to the convenience store a couple of blocks away from the house. I agreed, reluctantly. Later I rued letting her do my errand.

Jerry shook his head when I told him of the incident. "She has no sense of money values at all. I did not have the exact change so she took a dollar bill; and you know what she did? She spent the change on gum balls. Every penny! I couldn't believe my eyes when she opened her sweaty hand and I saw the stains. Thirty-three balls of bubble gum! All that she couldn't stuff in her mouth or hold in her hand, she dumped in the sack with the detergent. I asked why she didn't buy one and bring me the rest of the change. She said, 'I got rid of it.' That's all. She got rid of it!"

"We're out of ideas, Hon. I guess we'd better call and have the school make the necessary arrangements for more tests."

Jerry was right. We could not stall for time any longer. I made the call.

It was all cut and dried. The teacher set up an appointment at the local clinic. Joy rode with me to the big brick building while Jonathan played with the neighbor children.

Joy asked no questions. She may have considered it a part of her normal routine, but I'll never know. I circled the block a couple of times to work up the needed courage to enter the clinic. I held her hand tightly in mine as we walked inside.

A youngish man led her toward the testing area while the clinical psychologist scribbled notes as I retold our life story. Now and then he injected a question or pressed for details. I hoped this was the last such interview about Joy's erratic growth and behavior and the vague inconsistencies which characterized our child. It should have been easier for me this time, but it was equally difficult and little different from the first time. I knew, deep in my heart, that this was not the last such session.

After a couple of meetings, they said the tests were inconclusive and recommended counseling on a weekly basis; but after the second, Joy refused to return. She cried bitterly but never gave her reason. The psychologist agreed nothing would be gained if Joy would not talk with him, and counseling ceased.

Months later when we passed the clinic I asked her why she had not wanted to talk with the doctor. She seemed ashamed as she replied, "He asked me questions I don't know anything about." She quickly changed the subject to the evening's dinner menu.

Joy agreed to help set the table and did so, neatly and without a reminder! I thanked her and she startled me by saying, "I love you and Daddy and Jonathan so much, Mother. I'm glad God gave me such a nice family."

My eyes blurred as I stirred the gravy. I didn't think God had done her much of a favor. She was drifting aimlessly and we were doing nothing to help her. Then I heard her singing, slightly off key, "Jesus loves me, this I know, for the Bible tells me so."

"Thank you, dear God, for making Joy know that she is loved," I prayed. Then we four headed for the table. I silently added that prayer to the grace offered for the meal.

That night I thanked God again for her faith and trust in us and his love for Joy, and begged for guidance to keep her safe. I also thanked him for Jonathan's capabilities and understanding. He seemed older than Joy!

The wings of time seemed clipped as Joy remained stationary in her development. Her make-believe friend kept her from total loneliness and was her confidant. Joy tattled on herself, a habit which made discipline difficult. We had no desire to encourage lying about misbehavior, but there was a nagging doubt that Joy might be deliberately courting punishment. She never denied any misdeed.

Joy was too big to spank. We relied on lectures and the withholding of treats or favors, neither of which had much effect. Her reaction was, "I don't like it anyway," or "I didn't want to go there at all. I just said I did," or "I'm too fat anyway, put the old stuff in the garbage!"

Confining her to her room was definitely not the answer either. She spent too much time in her own company as it was. Joy appeared more and more oblivious to the world around her. She lived in her own private domain. Her summertime was filled with pretend activities, banging on the piano, and laughing at private jokes, which she was probably sharing with "She."

She would beg to go to the swimming pool, but when she got there she would sit in the shallow end and play with small children or splash—by herself. If she climbed to the top of the slide she wavered until some impatient youngster insisted she back down or pushed her down into the water, where she sprawled with a queen-size splash. Now and then she braved the ascent to the diving board, looked down, and then backed away. Obviously she was afraid. One evening she told us that she had jumped in, feet first, from the diving board—twice in one day! It must have required considerable time, motivation and courage.

I took time out from thinking of Joy's problems to

assess my own. I was slowly becoming a sidewalk psychiatrist, analyzing every word and deed. *That* would have to end!

Actually neither Jerry nor I knew much about how Joy really felt or what she thought. She was our enigma. She did things *her* way, ignoring advice, orders and the clock.

Time meant nothing. The large clock at the pool was meaningless, as were the wristwatches we bought for her. Usually she dawdled in the dressing room at the pool, watching the other girls dress or comb their hair and apply makeup. She paid no attention to her own appearance. She was bedraggled and unkempt when she finally emerged and sauntered to the car, apparently unaware that we were waiting in the blazing heat of July.

One particularly sweltering day I waited long after Jonathan had dressed and come to the car. The minute hand on the pool clock ticked steadily. "Joy is slow," the psychologist had said. Slow was hardly adequate! Both examinations had been wastes of time and money and only caused anguish. It wouldn't take a high-priced specialist to conclude that Joy was slow! It probably would do no good to try the local psychologist again, so I dismissed the thought.

But the thought would not remain dismissed as Joy's withdrawal and regression continued to dominate my days. Had we been told the whole truth? I was especially frightened when I read an article about schizophrenia, and decided to learn more about that mental illness and whether or not the affliction could be acquired or was inborn or hereditary.

Jerry was outraged by the suggestion. "Why put ideas in their heads?" He reminded me that I was no expert on mental illness and that I should stop "shooting at shadows." "Joy is O.K. She'll surprise all of us one of these days."

His words stung, but he was partly right. I was no expert and I could not view the situation objectively. But our disagreements were more frequent and sharper, and usually concerned Joy. Our life was far from ideal, and our marriage teetered on the brink of divorce. Both of our children deserved parental harmony and we were not giving it to them.

Jerry and I agreed a change of scenery might be good for the four of us. Disneyland's attractions sounded appealing, and a vacation would be therapeutic for everyone.

Jerry requested time off from his job and we headed west, away from the heat and usual routine. Joy slept in the back seat most of the way while Jonathan sat between Jerry and me, chattering about the things he saw along the highway.

Each night the motel was a fascinating experience for Joy. She went around the room examining the furniture, closets, pictures, and bathroom fixtures. She tested the beds, stood before the mirror, sat in each chair, and counted the motel rooms. We noticed her animation and were pleased.

Joy's more usual personality resurfaced when we reached our destination. Not even Disneyland could hold her attention long. Standing in line was not for our child. We couldn't let her wander away in the huge crowds, but neither were we able to restrain her physically. She began to cry loudly, like a small hurt child. We bypassed the rest of the attractions and returned to the car, well aware of the curious stares turned our way.

Joy climbed into the back seat, yawned noisily, and fell

fast asleep. Jonathan looked at her and then at us. He asked the question I had expected and dreaded. "What's wrong with Joy, Mother?"

"We don't know." I was almost glad not to have to explain some physical or mental problem. He seemed to be satisfied with my truthful reply and I wondered how long he would settle for such brief explanations. I was pleased that Jonathan did not pursue the subject. He was pretty big to sit on my lap, but he must have sensed my need to cuddle him and hold him tightly. I thanked God for my son.

Life was not fair to him, but nothing was fair or unfair anymore. Things were simply as they were. We couldn't do anything to change the situation, it seemed.

I repeated a couple of quotations which I had pasted on our dresser:

"There is no education like adversity" (Benjamin Disraeli). "Yield not to misfortunes but press forward the more boldly in their face" (Virgil).

They offered some comfort, as did Holy Scripture; but their soothing effects were waning as the years passed with no apparent solution to our problems. I did what I had done so often before. I prayed as we rode.

The present jerked me back from my reverie when Jonathan spied an ice cream stand and hamburger shop side by side, and Jerry stopped the car. Joy awakened, hungry and sweaty. The Disneyland experience was past and forgotten. She was smiling and happy, intent on a snack. It was ironic that Jonathan seemed older than teenage Joy.

Jerry had said nothing, his embarrassment greater than mine. The incident was not an everyday occurrence for him as it was for me, and it seemed to substantiate my complaints and fears.

Another afternoon we spent at the beach, and both children enjoyed the day. Joy was interested in the Marineland aquatic show for a while, and then became restless and bored. A sack of popcorn kept her quiet as we watched the remainder of the show.

Her lack of interest was nothing new and did not surprise me, but her comments did—while watching the dolphins' antics. She matter-of-factly told us she was going to have a formal wedding and twelve children—six boys and six girls. I shuddered and thought, "Heaven help us!" Then I recalled her recent demands for a bra and permission to date boys, and shivers spiraled up and down my spine. Clearly her mind was responding to her body's development. New problems were on our doorstep.

The vacation ended. Compared with others, it was a huge success. Joy occupied the "Pullman section," the back seat, most of the way home and young Jonathan liked the unaccustomed attention of both parents.

On our last night away from home, Jerry admitted he had not seen the situation clearly. "You're not making mountains out of molehills, after all. Guess we'd better get in touch with the last examiner and see if he has something to suggest now. It's not just for Joy. We can't keep on this way. I looked at the little fellow today, and Jonny deserves. . . ."

I cut in. "He deserves a normal life and he's not getting it! It's not *fair*! We can't think only of Joy and our stupid pride!"

"Right." He looked old and very, very tired. "Call the clinic the first thing Monday after we get home, and give them the go-ahead."

The last day on the road was long and hot, but we pushed on to reach home. The vacation had been an ordeal, but it had also put our marriage on a firmer footing.

Joy seemed anxious to be back in her own room. Could it be that home meant security for her? I shook off the role of analyst to resume being a wife and mother and housekeeper.

Jerry unloaded the car and I opened the windows wide before putting a load of laundry in the washer for a head start on the morning's chores. A cooling dish of ice cream before we tumbled into bed sounded appetizing. But while I dished up the treats, Joy disappeared. Her absence made me a bit jittery and I called to her to come for ice cream. She said that she had checked on the washer and I forgot the incident.

The next morning when I went to the basement, the floor and machine were covered with dried soapsuds. She had dumped a whole box of detergent in the washer again. Her stock answer when she had done this in the past had been that she had "gotten rid of it." She never knew her reason but always promised she would never ever do it again.

Remnants of doubts about the need of counseling vanished as I worked at cleaning up the mess. She was not progressing. She was not even standing still. She was regressing.

The following week Joy and I drove to the clinic while Jonathan played with his best friend. He had a key to the house and would make a sandwich if we had not returned by noon. His ability to take care of himself was a godsend.

Joy said nothing as we entered the building or when the clinical psychologist greeted us. Then an aide led her to another room and I proceeded to the psychologist's domain. There was nothing to gain by hiding any unpleasant facts, so I told him frankly that it seemed things had been bad when we contacted him initially, but that they had gotten progressively worse. He took it in stride. I warned him to give her an entirely different battery of tests as she had memorized the ink blots and other devices after her first examination.

It was not intended as a joke, but he laughed. "There's nothing wrong with her memory!"

"That's part of the trouble. Why can't she remember the things we try to teach her, yet recall minute details from maps or pictures? We've worked hard to have her help with the dishes or vacuum the floor or iron the flatwork, but she makes a big mess of everything. Even napkins! I have to do them over because she absolutely will not use both hands. I tried having her do her own blouses and things, but you wouldn't believe how they looked.

"I attended a P.T.A. meeting a few years ago. The speaker, a child psychiatrist, said that ambidextrous children receive their motor guidance from both lobes of the brain. Joy is definitely ambidextrous."

He tapped a pencil thoughtfully. "If Joy were my child, I'd try to set up an appointment with the Menninger Foundation in Topeka, Kansas. There are so many contradictions. I am convinced she is not retarded, but neither is she normal. In some respects she seems to be feebleminded. Frankly, her problem—whatever it is—is not going to disappear by itself and will only grow worse."

Menninger's? Wasn't that a place for crazy people? Why there? Did he think Joy was mentally ill? None of the questions would come out, and I began to cry. I did ask if she might be schizophrenic.

"I don't know, but I doubt it. Menninger's can tell you. I recommend them highly."

"But what will we tell her? Or the neighbors and our friends? Or Jonathan?"

"Don't talk about it. She will know, but it's nobody's business. Forget other people. Forget nosy neighbors. And be brief when you tell Jonathan."

I fought the step internally. The doctor must have read my mind. "Ask another psychologist if you want another opinion. That's fine with me. But bear in mind, you have two children to consider and there are four people involved. Tests can't hurt Joy. They might help all four of you."

Struggling for composure, I told him we would discuss it and let him know in a few days. I doubted Jerry would agree to Menninger's.

"By the way, Mrs. Jennings, you should know that Joy scored in the mid-80s in the I.Q. test."

"Mid-80s? We thought...."

"I know. These tests do vary and are not conclusive."

There was nothing left to say, and he sent for Joy and bade us goodbye. It was fortunate that there was little traffic. As I drove, Joy looked at me questioningly and I dreaded her asking for details of my conference. What a surprise when she said, "Mother, have you got hay fever? Your eyes are all red and funny looking."

"Guess so, Honey. How about helping fix dinner to-night?"

She thought it was a great idea and decided we would serve hamburgers and carrot salad and that she would bake a cake. The menu presented no problem and I had a box of chocolate mix on hand. Why not let her try? It would boost her ego.

When we reached the house, I discovered there were no eggs in the refrigerator. Joy preferred to stay home while I drove to the market. Although the errand took only a few minutes, when I returned the house smelled strongly of chocolate. Joy had become impatient and sub-stituted a cup of water for two eggs. The result was a gooey cross between pudding and gravy.

A few bites were all we could eat. But Joy seemed not to mind until she saw it in the garbage. Then she laughed hilariously.

After we tucked the children in bed, Jerry and I talked until late. We had to make a decision *now*. But testing at Menninger's amounted to betrayal. We decided we would look elsewhere for help. Meanwhile, we would spend more time with Joy, and more time with the Lord. I would say nothing to anyone, and continue to act as if there was nothing wrong at home. When other people were near, Joy's eccentric behavior would receive no attention, no matter what it was. I would *not* see questioning looks. Unnecessary contact with the parents of the children Joy's age was out, as was the P.T.A. Church attendance and Sunday school were ordeals, but essential. We lived by a double set of standards.

After one particularly unpleasant day I told Jerry I was not cut out to be a martyr, and broke into tears. I knew self-pity was a waste of time and energy, but the slightest expression of sympathy brought on weeping sessions. Our 24 hours a day of tension was a lifestyle that took its toll.

Sermons seemed to be written for my ears and edification and some became intolerable. To shut them out, I recited David's psalm, "The Lord is my shepherd, I shall not want. He maketh me to lie down in green pastures. . . ." I tried to believe that the Lord was offering me comfort.

One sermon concluded that according to James 2:1 the ground at the foot of Jesus' cross is level and all humanity is treated equally. Equality through distribution of talents was the interpretation he gave to I Corinthians 12:12, 27.

The combined references and Psalm 23 seemed to mock me. I was almost an agnostic now; my burden was becoming heavier than my faith could carry.

chapter **6**

Perhaps JUNIOR HIGH SCHOOL would change Joy's behavior. But we hesitated to be optimistic as we recalled the letdowns of the past.

Joy selected new clothes and school supplies carefully. I eyed the gym uniform, wondering if she would change into it and then back into her regular clothes and be on time for her next class. I knew that the presence of other girls slowed her to a standstill.

Getting Joy to and from school was also a worry. The doctors had said she must be independent. She wanted to ride her bicycle, but she refused to get on it until we removed the training wheels. We then learned that several younger boys had teased her about her "tricycle."

We worked long hours on her balance. She wobbled and fell, got up, and wobbled and fell again many times. Her elbows and knees were covered with bandages, but we were glad her injuries were only scrapes and bruises. She persisted and eventually rode alone. But the night she soloed, Joy broke out in a rash of hives. The doctor attributed it to nervousness.

Joy's first day in junior high was a huge success. She rode her bike to school. Her hair was still neat and shining when she returned and her eyes sparkled. She had not picked out the hem of her new skirt. She talked about her teachers and the various rooms and about how fast she had walked to avoid being tardy. Jerry and I basked in the heady glow.

Then Joy candidly asked, "Am I pregnant, Mother?"

When we had recovered our aplomb, I stammered that she certainly was *not* pregnant. "Why do you ask?" I tried to keep the panic from my voice.

A couple of girls in her gym class had apparently noticed her protruding abdomen and said she was pregnant. So our earlier facts-of-life talk had not served its purpose.

Jerry shook his head and said dryly, "Never a dull moment!"

That night we decided we had to take Joy to the Menninger Foundation.

We were able to set up an appointment for two months later, and departed in the car as furtively as burglars. Thunderheads made the dreary trip even drearier; and when loud thunderclaps and a pelting rain added their dismal touches, my thoughts returned to Good Friday, 1944. Bad weather was merely coincidental, I rationalized.

Jonathan snuggled closer to me as lightning bolts brightened the sky, but Joy slept soundly in the back seat as usual. When we reached a motel late that afternoon, she ran ahead of us to avoid being soaked. She darted around, counting the stationery in the desk, four small bars of soap, four hand towels, four bath towels, and four washcloths. I counted too—the number of hours until our first appointment at the clinic! I prayed that we would finally get some answers.

It was still raining in the morning as we continued our drive to Topeka. The time for our initial contact was 1 P.M. We ate an early lunch and then headed for the maze of formidable buildings housing the world-famed clinic. Some were old and renovated houses; others were modern brick office and dormitory-type buildings. Many of the hardwood trees were already bare of leaves, their skeletal forms adding to the overall gloom of our trip.

"Hold my hand, Jerry. I'm not sure I can make it up those steps alone," I whispered.

His voice was harsh and grim as he said, "Come on, Jane," and I realized it was that way much of the time these days. "Here we go again."

We were committed, I thought to myself. Then I shuddered at the ugly image. Committed! Mental illness. Confinement. Would Joy be committed? I wanted to run and never stop but that was impossible. There was no way back. All four J. J.s entered the waiting room.

We sat with Jonathan while a specialist gave Joy a preliminary examination. Another old-looking young couple shared the room with us. They, too, had a hopeless and dull expression. Forty-five slow-moving minutes dragged by, and then a sitter appeared to stay with Jonathan. He didn't question us, but seemed to understand that we had a problem and cooperated. I wondered what was going on in his mind, and was grateful that he did not quiz us. The course of events was making an old man of our little boy; and I hated it with a passion while thanking God for sparing us comparable problems with him.

We crossed the yard to a small cottage where we began a series of several days' interviews, in-depth probings spanning every phase of Joy's existence from conception to that day.

Joy's tests included puzzle-working, interpretation of ink blots and pictures, and a complete physical. The last examination was a brain wave test, electroencephalograph. The wires the attendant glued to Joy's head frightened her, and she screamed for me to hold her tightly. I stroked her arms and kissed her tenderly, waiting for a sedative to calm her. Soon Joy fell asleep, and I tiptoed to the anteroom.

I could watch her through a large glass window. A strange looking machine stood beside me and the attendant. She flipped a switch and tape began spewing from the instrument as a number of "pens" started to mark the paper. Jagged lines formed, recording Joy's brain waves. Two of the series of lines differed radically from the others. I sensed this was important and wondered why they were so erratic. "That's not right," I said to the attendant. She said she was not in a position to read the results but that a neurologist would interpret the markings. My throat seemed dry and my dress was choking me. My eyes remained glued to the rolling paper and those two deviant lines.

I dared not let Joy see my fear, and there was nothing to be gained by scaring Jerry. Those inked test results might not mean anything bad. I was no technician and obviously knew nothing of "normal" lines, so there was no reason to panic.

Soon the test ended and the machine stopped. Through the window I saw Joy stirring, and hurried to her side. She yawned and opened her eyes. She began to sob when she realized where she was. Finally she quieted and asked, "Do I have to take any more tests?"

I shook my head and she added, "I hope not! Anyway, they gave me the same old tests. Why don't they get some new ones?"

I gasped. Then the impact of her remark hit. How much of the week's testing had she carried in her memory?

Our final conference was set for the next morning. Jerry and I were impatient, hopeful and fearful. As we entered the waiting room, the same couple we had seen the previous day sat on the other side of the small room, waiting for their last meeting with the doctors. Their twelve-year-old was engrossed in a comic book.

He was over six feet tall! Joy too at thirteen was already several inches taller than I and outweighed me by about thirty pounds, I realized with a jolt.

I felt vaguely comfortable with this unknown couple we would probably never see again. Her hair was almost as gray as mine! Ah, blessed anonymity. *They* knew what none of our friends or relatives knew—we were having Joy examined for mental defects.

A counselor and a psychiatrist sat with us in a semicircle around a desk in the familiar conference room. In a businesslike manner the counselor began, "We have pooled the results of our diversified tests." She wasted no time. I took a deep breath. "Some of Joy's previous I.Q. scores indicate a range of nearly 30 points—from 75 to 103. We feel she is in the mid-80 range. That is within normal boundaries."

"I *knew* she wasn't retarded," I interrupted.

She nodded. "That's right. She is not retarded. She is what we call a 'borderline.' You two must accept her as she is and stop trying to fit her into your mold. She *cannot* make it! Remove her from competitive situations

and don't fuss so much about her appearance and mannerisms. You're hurting her by forcing her to conform beyond
her capacity. She evidently realizes and worries about the
fact that she is different."

"Different, but how?" I doubted that I would ever be
able to ignore Joy when she picked at her nose and then
put her finger in her mouth, or scratched herself in public,
or belched noisily. I could not mask her behavior, and she
could not—or would not—change. Did it really matter if
strangers or acquaintances saw her childlike actions? It
was both naive and stupid to think people would not know
Joy had a problem and was "different." But Joy did not
have the usual identifying marks of retardation.

She was *not* retarded, but her problem was as serious
as any retardate's. I wanted to scream for help as I looked
to see how Jerry was taking the diagnosis. Morbid
thoughts converted the conference into an inquest—an
autopsy.

The counselor's voice jerked me back to the present,
and I reached for another tissue. The psychologist and
psychiatrist detailed the results in clinical terms. They
proved the damning verdict—borderline retardation, minimal brain dysfunction, brain damage, central nervous
system irregularity.

We sat quietly and heard our high hopes for Joy
plummet. Our perfect little girl was not so perfect after
all. Dreams, hopes, goals, false pride—all crashed in a
miserable heap, with jagged splinters to cut and scar us.
"Begin again from point zero. There's no way but up," a
friend had uttered years ago when her entire family had
been killed in an automobile crash.

We hit bottom when the counselor told Jerry, "She has

probably progressed as far as she can. She will always be your 'little girl.' She is about at the end of any real achievement in school. Her central nervous system is damaged. Two lobes of her brain have not fully developed, probably because of some prenatal defect."

Two lobes? Two? Those jagged lines on the machine tape. . . . "What caused it? How do you know?" I asked.

"The neurological examination indicates an early injury, verified by the E.E.G. test. Her tied tongue and her foot deformities tend to verify the diagnosis."

"You mean the unusually high arches?"

"Yes, and also there is little or no protective padding over the metatarsal bones. Didn't you know that both of her feet are affected this way?"

He couldn't believe earlier tests hadn't revealed this fact. "We can't pinpoint the cause of the brain injury, but we suspect the flu you had early in your pregnancy. You mustn't blame yourselves or anyone else. It is nothing she inherited, and it could happen to anyone. Believe me, there are hundreds of thousands of babies born with similar disabilities and much worse."

"But why? Why Joy?" He shrugged his shoulders and I continued. "I've never seen anyone like her. None of the tests. . . . None of the doctors we've taken her to. . . . What can we do to correct it?"

"Nothing."

"Nothing? Surely there's some surgery or medicine or therapy or something. . . ." Jerry's voice sounded flat and lifeless as he groped for encouragement.

"I'm afraid there's nothing that can be done to correct the brain damage. You'll have to learn to live with it, and accept her as she is."

Nothing. No hope at all. Our poor little girl. Why did it happen to her? And what would happen to her in the future? She was so trusting. Perhaps if we helped her a great deal, she could become a normal adult.

My next question was foolish and silly, and the counselor was kind not to chide me. "No, Mrs. Jennings. I could be wrong, but I recommend Joy never marry. If she were to have children, she could not cope with them." (No argument there!) "And another thing, boys may prove to be a big source of trouble. She does not look handicapped and she is pretty. She also is very much interested in boys now. She has normal instincts. You must protect her from the ones who would take advantage of her gullibility. Protect her from them—and from herself. She is too trusting for her own good, and could be an easy mark."

She had answered an unasked question, and she was right about Joy's blind trust. She had never met a stranger, an enemy, a cheat or a liar.

They recommended a change in Joy's school situation but special education was not indicated. That was good, I thought, for none was available in the small town we called home. Joy's memory would help her as it had in the past, but she could not ever be expected to achieve in competition. "Avoid comparison with other youngsters."

"Is she schizophrenic?" I *had* to know.

"No."

I had read an article about brain injuries and aphasia. Children, it said, were being trained to use another lobe of the brain to perform the lost capabilities. The psychiatrist said treatment of that kind was not possible in Joy's case.

One point bothered me, although I felt their clinical diagnoses were right. "Is it possible she began with extraordinarily high intelligence? Otherwise, how could she function as well as she does?"

"Yes. There is a possibility she would have been the genius child you thought she was. But there's no way to tell."

That knowledge salved my wounded pride. But it wouldn't change anything. What was so great about being a genius? I hated myself for hunting for face-savers. I was a stupid old woman!

When there was nothing more to discuss, the counselor handed Jerry a directory of schools and residential facilities for handicapped children. "You may need this. Most libraries stock it or you may wish to buy a copy."

Jerry looked at it briefly and returned it with a wry smile. "Thanks, but we'll manage some other way. We'll keep her at home and take care of her the best we can."

The woman hesitated a second. Then she said, "Joy is very worried about herself. She senses she is different and knows she disappoints you when she brings home bad grades. She is ashamed of her poor report cards. She doesn't understand herself. So take it easy with her. And try not to let her see your concern. It won't be easy. But you *absolutely must relax*—for the sake of your entire family!"

We nodded in unison.

"One last thing. Don't 'kill her with kindness.' She's smart and is apt to take advantage of you if you give her half a chance."

"What can we tell her about her problem?"

"Don't tell her anything. It would only hurt her because she wouldn't understand and you'd be sorry you'd opened your mouth. There's no end once you get the ball rolling, and it's all downhill. It is definitely best that she never know the clinical findings. But relax—for everyone's sake."

Many of our whys had been answered. The counselor commented, "Nietzsche said that he who has a 'why' to live for can bear almost any 'how.'"

We said our goodbyes and left. Some of the answers were far from what we had hoped for, but the idea of considering four people instead of one gained importance. Undoubtedly Jonathan had been hurt, although he gave no indication. I recalled the words of our friend, Dr. Charley, when Jonathan was only ten months old. "He's way ahead of himself and he'll have lots of problems adjusting to kids his own age. Don't hold him back but don't push him either. Extremes of any kind are hard to handle intelligently. You may have your hands full, Janey."

Jonathan was in kindergarten and loved it. Right now our number one priority was Joy's school situation. There was but one school in town. Keeping her up with the class would be my task.

We sloshed through the rain to the reception office and then to the car, with both children in tow. I hated the rain! Why did it always pour when we had a crisis? It seemed ominous.

A forecast for snow and freezing temperatures did not change our decision to head for home. We checked out of the motel, filled the gas tank, and began the long homeward trek.

Jerry said nothing as he drove. His jaw was still clenched and rigid as it had been during the conference, moving occasionally as if he were grinding ugly, unspoken words into nothingness.

Riding in silence, I admitted we should have recognized some of the signs the doctors had used to verify their findings. The invisible shield which she had built around herself was a protective barrier. Being almost normal, Joy was a study in conflict. She could not make and then live with decisions, and she was aware of her shortcomings.

The idea that Joy's brain might be damaged had not occurred to us, and apparently had eluded the various doctors who had examined her previously; but surely someone should have suspected some such condition.

Joy was bound to ask questions which I could not dodge—or answer. Should I lie to her? Skip over issues? It would only hurt her to know the details of her handicap, they had said. What made them so sure? Maybe their diagnosis was inaccurate, or perhaps they were not 100 percent sure. Could they be guessing? Perhaps brain damage was an out for them. Other doctors had never even suggested it. But they had not given her an E.E.G. test either—with two squiggly lines different from the rest.

Brain damage. Brain damage. Central nervous system. Over and over they pounded, keeping time with the monotonous swishing of the windshield wipers. My head was splitting!

Joy's sobbing interrupted my morbidity, and I asked, "What is it, Honey?" She did not reply, crying louder and louder until Jerry stopped the car and I moved to the back seat with her. "I dreamed you were dead," she finally said. She touched my cheek, held my hand, and kissed me. To verify that I was alive? Then in an angry voice she said, "If you ever die or leave me, I'll kill you!"

We cried together. I had already broken my promise not to weep in front of her or Jonathan.

Poor little girl. Poor little boy. He had never received his share of attention and he was such a sweet little fellow. I shivered. Had we known of Joy's affliction, we would not have had him lest he too might suffer some handicap. How glad I was that we had been ignorant of the injury!

Joy dozed again.

"Accept her as she is. Stop trying to fit her into your mold." It was easy for them to say. They were not involved. "There is nothing we can do to correct her condition. You'll have to learn to live with it—and her." Their words spun in my head, and I asked God for help and extra strength. "She is ashamed...." Poor, poor little girl. "She is not retarded." I wanted to shout it, savoring the crumbs of the slice of cake which could not be mine.

When "normal" kids passed us I would look the other way, and when their smug mothers bragged about perfect report cards and successes or victories I would smile, but I would hate them. Keep up a good appearance. Be an ostrich. What a hypocrite I would be, but no one would ever be able to quote *me* about Joy's condition.

Shivering, I recalled the Scriptures. "The sins of the fathers shall be visited upon...." Who was responsible? How far back lay the sin? Why had God punished my innocent little girl? Or was it the obstetrician's fault? The anaesthetic he gave me was too strong, or too much. Why did he lie to us and say Joy was perfect? Did he suspect something was wrong and try to cover up some mistake? Did the first psychologist know? Or did we not understand him because of his accent? No. He would have made us understand. All he said was that Joy was slow. Had he meant mentally instead of physically? Had Joy—and her memory—fooled everyone? How about her teachers? And could Jerry and I handle whatever developed? How long could we continue pretending we were a normal family? God, help us! *Please!*

Jonathan seemed to sense our troubles and was quiet as we rode. I kissed his forehead, happy that he was still young enough not to object. He needed mothering, and I needed him.

All of us needed to eat something. It was getting dark and the roads were beginning to freeze, but Jerry preferred to drive the entire distance without stopping overnight in a motel. After dinner the children slept, so I could cry as much as I wanted. Jerry kept his eyes on the road, his jaw frozen into an unmoving brake on his emotions lest they spill and overflow reason.

"Jerry. If the school can't change things . . . and if we can't handle the situation . . . what'll we do? Will we have to put her in an. . . ."

He cut me off shortly. "Don't *ever* say that word! You hear me? *Nothing* could ever make me do that to her. *Nothing. Never!*"

We clung tenaciously to the fragment of hope that we could somehow handle the situation ourselves, and that Joy would eventually overcome her problem. And *if* the diagnosis proved incorrect, as had previous tests, Joy's life might be almost normal. Maybe some medication or surgical technique could be developed to repair the damage which had been done to Joy's brain, compared to a defective electric cord that short-circuited when the contact was not exactly on target. Breakthroughs were being written up all the time in medical journals. Nothing was impossible.

If the diagnosis proved wrong, and if Joy merely needed individual instruction I might be able to help her over her hurdles while guiding her schoolwork. I had aspired to be a teacher and perhaps my tutoring would do the job. We could live together as a family.

The obvious drawbacks to this arrangement were too much mothering for me and not enough self-reliance for Joy. And it would be difficult to conceal my pity for Joy's handicapped state and avoid being overly protective or hypersensitive to reactions to her odd behavior and re-marks. I dreaded facing curious friends and acquaintances.

That first week back home we were tempted to skip Sunday school and church, but we went. We struggled to be on time and I even helped Joy dress. Her dawdling should not have irritated me, but it did. Obviously I needed divine guidance plus a morale booster. The clinicians' impersonal advice was totally unrealistic!

Jerry squared his jaw and held his head a bit higher as we neared the church. He, too, showed the strain. Happily, no one mentioned our week's absence from town or our hollow eyes and their dark encircling shadows. I didn't notice anyone staring at Joy or us. Perhaps her eccentricities were less noticeable to outsiders than we feared. My errant thoughts roamed far afield as the service continued. I wondered what lay ahead for us and prayed to God for help.

Joy hummed "The Lord's Prayer" as we drove home, in her slightly off-key way. Suddenly she stopped and asked what we were having for dinner. "Roast beef," I replied.

After the fourth identical question and answer I told her sharply not to ask again.

"I only wanted to know what we're having for dinner. You don't have to get mad about it!"

She was right. Losing my temper was unnecessary and I bit my tongue, promising to try harder. Jerry scowled and Jonathan looked embarrassed as Joy repeated her criticism and explanation a couple more times.

Self-hatred and self-pity grew increasingly pervasive as the day wore on, and my feeble attempts at normalcy withered. Joy agreed to dry the dinner dishes; still she headed for the bathroom and a long, jolly visit with "She." Much later, without being reminded, she put each air-dried dish in the cupboard, neatly, and in its rightful place.

She telephoned a classmate to invite her to our house. The girl declined and Joy begged and then became belligerent, demanding reasons why she would not come to visit. She was puzzled when the girl hung up on her. She went through her identical routine with three more girls; and after the last call appeared somewhat elated as she walked to the calendar, flipped the pages to July, and then asked what date would be the seventh Saturday in July, because that was the day Cindy was coming over and Joy could not locate in on the calendar. No reply would have been suitable; and when none was forthcoming, Joy shrugged and went to watch a televised cartoon. She and her "friend" had another lively conversation before she went to bed, early as usual.

Two days had passed. Joy had not mentioned the clinic, the examinations or the trip. It was as if the week had not existed. I dreaded the questions she might one day ask concerning herself. It seemed imperative that we follow Menninger's advice. But issues must be dodged if we were to avoid revealing the true nature of her handicap. Her blind faith would make it easier now, but what about in five or ten years?

There was no way to avoid revealing her affliction to the school principal and teachers. And so I told them the unembellished truth—plus the fact that Joy was *not* retarded, and begged for understanding, tolerance and help. Everyone agreed to cooperate and avoid placing Joy in competitive situations as much as possible. We would work as a team, guided by Joy's needs.

I implored their secrecy, but perhaps the teachers told their friends and relatives the details of the testing. I'll never know. The only other person I confided in was our pastor and personal friend. His broad shoulder offered solace, and his prayers added to ours might get us through to God. Mine alone were not enough. I also contacted our family physician for a sedative, and gave "bad news from my family" as the cause of my need.

The tranquilizers permitted me to sleep and handle the many demands on my time and energy. Joy and I studied together until ten each evening, in line with our plan. We read the lessons word by word to complete assignments. Algebra required long sessions although she memorized the formulae quickly and solved some of the problems readily. History was easy when it involved dates and lists of things to commit to memory. English was more difficult. Joy seemed unable to differentiate between nouns, pronouns and verbs. Once identified, she breezed through diagramming sentences.

The more relaxed academic schedule plus her completed homework appeared to be succeeding, and our collective hopes zoomed. Trivialities became major victories. However, before long Joy tired earlier and completed less and less of the total assignments. Evening study sessions became ordeals dreaded by both of us, and were rivaled only by the effort of getting her out of bed in the morning, dressed and off to school on time.

She began awakening daily with a stomachache, a toothache, a headache or a sore back muscle. And once in school, she spent much time in the nurse's office on a cot, suffering from some ache or pain.

Changing clothes for physical education was a particular irritant, and Joy was tardy to her next class most of the time. She frequently neglected to bring home her soiled gym uniform for laundering and commenced forgetting her books or the necessary tools to do her homework. Each day something was misplaced at school. Joy's remarkable memory seemed to have deserted her.

The complexities of junior high school bewildered our child; and as her confusion grew, so grew her frustration. "Why don't the other kids like me?" "Why don't they invite me to their parties?" "Why don't the boys ask me for dates?" "Why do you keep staring at me, Mother? Is there something wrong with me? And why do you cut onions all the time? You know they make you cry."

Her moods were as varying as a weathervane. Violent tears and angry tirades alternated with moody and quiet days when she seemed lost in space. Twice she barely escaped being struck down as she absentmindedly stepped in front of cars; but she seemed unaware of the danger, complaining instead that their screeching tires hurt her ears. She was withdrawn and uncommunicative. She rarely touched the piano except to pound the keys viciously now and then, venting stored-up fury at some unnamed person or thing. Joy, who had always anticipated Sunday school and church, began to find excuses to stay at home. She was too tired or she didn't feel well or she had made arrangements to visit a friend. Anything served as a reason.

Her behavior was totally unpredictable. She became bellicose and surly and her actions more juvenile. Explaining the meanings of obscene gestures and words and profanities had little effect. Joy elected to copy what she saw and heard in the halls at school, much as she had done as a toddler in her playpen. And, now as then, she taunted me, repeating the ugly words over and over, daring me to punish her. "Be gentle with her. Don't magnify unimportant things," the doctors had said; but their advice was difficult to follow. Several times I even spanked her, the only punishment I knew how to inflict.

How would the professionals react to pinholes which let thin rivulets of toothpaste squish onto their hands, or a paste made of expensive gift cologne and bath powder and water, or clothes riddled with holes after being doused with undiluted bleach, or a half full bottle of shampoo being refilled with water, or an entire box of detergent clogging the dishwasher and engulfing the kitchen in suds? I doubted they could remain calm and gentle in our everyday crises.

Joy was now a definite discipline problem. She became more tyrannical daily. The mandate for motherhood did not come complete with directions to handle children like Joy! I developed a guilt complex and hated myself for ugly thoughts and acts. Joy seemed to sense my unwillingness to punish her, and took advantage of my willy-nillyness.

Jerry and I argued constantly over the handling of our affairs. Divorce was imminent. It dangled the temptation of having to find a job to support the children while relieving me of the twenty-four-hour mothering which caged me. Jerry's level head set me straight. Jonathan and Joy needed two parents, and my problems would multiply tenfold without another adult for companionship. Many times I believed God had deserted us and that there was no point in struggling against our plight. We made no decisions with confidence.

After one particularly bad day Jerry and I talked long into the night, not arguing or blaming each other for a change. We avoided the word "institutionalization" which haunted us and kept us awake at night, but that word had gradually acquired a new significance since our session at Menninger's.

Joy was steadily regressing. She had received failure notices in all but one subject, and it was apparent that her needs were not being met in school. We could not move to another town and we were, after all, being forced to give Joy into the care of strangers. We could not yet voice the word "institutionalization." Placement sounded better.

We had read too many accounts of the horrendous treatment of persons with handicaps in institutions and knew the blanket indictment of parents who placed their children instead of keeping them at home. The world of mental illness, however, has many ramifications, and we were at last able to conclude that there just might be institutions that could do more with Joy than we were able to do.

chapter 7

THE DECISION to place Joy was difficult. Even more difficult was putting our decision into effect. We had no idea how to proceed.

Then we remembered the suggestion of the counselor at the Menninger Foundation, and we obtained a copy of the Porter Sargent directory. Each day while Joy was at school I studied the listings of homes and schools, individual requirements, facilities, and costs. We did not seem to fit any of the pigeonholes. No facilities were listed for brain-damaged borderlines. Nor was there anything close to our home. Joy was too old for most of the homes, and we were neither rich enough nor poor enough. Had Joy been blind, deaf, cardiac, orthopedically handicapped, retarded, Mongoloid, emotionally disturbed, schizophrenic, cerebral palsied, spastic, or bedfast we could have chosen from several residential schools.

After rereading the directory I decided to write to several institutions in neighboring states. I outlined Joy's condition and asked for information. I also sought guidance from government agencies at all levels and from local parent groups.

Four residential schools sent literature and application

forms. One was equipped to handle all types of exceptional children. I read their brochure until the words were blurred and fuzzy. Clear thinking was essential, I reminded myself angrily. Crying would never solve the problem!

None of the four sounded exactly right. We had to see the facilities and talk with the people in charge before we made any decisions. Jerry arranged for long weekends, and we scheduled trips which took us to the Midwest and the Southwest, treating each jaunt as a vacation. I told Joy we were looking for a boarding school which she might enjoy more than her present school. She did not question the action, but now I am confident she understood more than we suspected. I had guilt pangs at the time, ashamed of my deceit. At nearly fourteen, Joy was as trusting as a small child. She had to be protected!

The four "homes" differed radically, from unspeakable to beautiful, and from low-priced to exorbitant. Joy would never fit into the bleak converted warehouse with its adult-sized furniture labeled "table" and "chair," and so forth. The long tables and stark furnishings in the dining room sent shivers over my body.

Nor would we leave her in the old farmhouse with its steep stairs and antequated plumbing, where bedrooms now serve as classrooms and the girls are housed in a large second-story room, barracks fashion, with boys in an adjacent building. A wave of near nausea swept over me as we approached a cluster of about ten girls of assorted ages and sizes. They did nothing and said nothing. They merely sat quietly, except for two hyperactive children at the end of the room who moved constantly. The uniformed attendant was busy with a basket of mending and a soap opera's star wept and screamed on a blaring TV. Joy said not one word as she followed our lead.

The next, a new and beautifully furnished ranch-type school-home would have been satisfactory except that it was priced way above our means. We were forced to eliminate the fourth, a dreary red brick building. Its cutoff age was thirteen.

Our pro-and-con emotions included relief at not having to part with Joy and distress at our inability to find a suitable place for her. As we neared home, Jerry said, "From what we've seen, we'd better try harder to make things work at home."

"It makes me sick. What do they expect parents to do with the kids after they reach twelve or fifteen or eighteen? They need help as much as the little ones. We can't just bury Joy."

He agreed it would have been simpler had we known earlier what Joy's problem was, and if she were more seriously handicapped. It seemed that being a borderline was more of a problem than being truly retarded.

We read the directory again, focusing on homes previously bypassed due to their distance from home, and decided to visit one. The large, farm-type group of buildings offered separate dormitories for boys and girls, a central building for meals and recreation, and separated classrooms. Large trees and spacious lawns promised breathing room, and the food which was served cafeteria style was prepared in a clean and modern kitchen. The supervised youngsters ranged in age from pre-school to early twenties, and they were busy in group play or watching television. Parties and social affairs were described as regular occurrences. Schooling to match capa-

bilities would be available on a non-competitive basis; and
housing would be with girls of comparable I.Q. and handicap.

We tried hard to govern our elation. Joy was anxious
to attend this "boarding school." And we felt this might be
the right place for Joy, at least for the time being. We
asked to be placed on the waiting list, and headed home to
discipline our thinking and work out a new budget.

The extensive wardrobe required by the school included lightweight and heavy coats, sweaters, twelve school
dresses, two Sunday dresses, a formal with accessories,
various shoes, shorts, slacks, blouses, and two swimsuits.
Joy was excited as I pinned and fitted her first evening
dress, wriggling and squirming steadily as I marked the
hem. Finally the pale green net-over-satin formal was
completed, and Joy modeled it for Jerry. It was just the
right color for her unusual eyes and burnished auburn
hair, which shone in the light like a thousand carats of
beauty. As Jerry photographed the pretty sight, my mind
raced to similar scenes in the past. I wondered again why
this beautiful child had to suffer.

It was easy to be maudlin. Many times I hid and wept
in solitude. I still secretly wondered if schizophrenia could
develop from her continual rejection and frustration. Surely the "home" would know and care for her if that proved
to be the case.

Months passed before the school notified us that a
room was available for Joy. Her clothing requirements
were complete and we shopped for her linens: a dozen
towels, two pillows, six sheets and pillow cases, winter
and summer blankets and two washable bedspreads.

Joy appeared to be anxious to leave, and the four of us

drove to her new home. There we signed a contract for one year's residential schooling and care. Jerry and I prayed this was not another in our long list of mistakes.

She wandered around the huge living room, noting the furnishings and decoration, and meeting various girls of assorted ages and both obvious and concealed handicaps. She stared at some of the more grotesquely misshapen residents but said nothing. What was going through her mind? I wondered.

It seemed most opportune that the home was having a formal party that night and Joy could wear her new dress. Her eyes lit up and danced in anticipation of attending a boy-and-girl party. I hoped it would be well-chaperoned!

When all of her paraphernalia was unpacked and in the office for name-tagging, we kissed Joy and prepared to leave for home in accordance with the superintendent's recommendation. We would not be permitted to see her again for ninety days; and the similarity between this orientation period and a jail sentence struck me. Through letters we would learn her reaction to the party, the other girls and boys, and living away from home.

Leaving was easier while she was engrossed in becoming acquainted and oblivious to our departure. She didn't even turn to wave goodbye.

As we rode homeward in silence, many unanswerable questions crossed and recrossed my mind, alternating with prayers. Jerry drove as if in a trance, his face drawn and taut. Was he also wondering if we had made the right decision? Why could we not cope with the problem ourselves? And when I saw jagged streaks of lightning far ahead I wondered what would happen when Joy became frightened of a pending electrical storm.

Would someone soothe and calm her? Would someone comfort her if she awakened with memories of a nightmare and cried in terror or anguish? What if she became ill? Would she miss us after the newness of the home wore off, and would she be homesick? Who would help Joy dress for tonight's party? Would she have a good time? Would some of the boys ask her to dance? Would she make friends or would she rely on her "friend" to share her new home and new lifestyle?

I shook myself. There was nothing to do about it now. Joy would be independent of me, as she *had to be*. I wouldn't live forever to make her decisions and think for her. "Help her, God, please, and *please* help me stop this silly crying! Jonathan must not be subjected to such a dismal life, and he must not be smothered with too much attention either. He's a 'lonely only' now. Please, dear God, help all four of us."

"Mother, why is Joy going to live there with those funny-looking girls?" Jonathan's question yanked me back to the present. Too much explanation was unnecessary, but lying to him was out of the question. "She'll be happier there. It is a boarding school." Technically speaking, it was the truth. "Institutionalization" was still a word banned from our vocabulary, and retardation in any degree was a shameful stigma. Jerry glanced sideways. He said nothing but tears showed in his eyes.

Jerry seemed to be reading my mind. "If she's sick or hurt, the nurse will get in touch with us immediately." The monthly progress report should also keep us posted on her health, but I wondered just as much about her happiness.

The first such report advised that Joy was adjusting nicely and seemed happy and healthy. Joy's first letter to us, a class project, was written under supervision. It told us little about her activities; it was, however, grammatically correct and spelled and punctuated perfectly.

The first bill provided an unpleasant shock. In addition to the regular monthly fee there were charges for textbooks and supplies and assorted extras that were deemed necessary to Joy's welfare. The letter also included a list of clothing and linens needed to replace unmendable items Joy had ripped into strips. Our already strained budget barely covered the total—almost half again as much as we had allotted. It also recommended speech therapy for Joy.

We came to dread opening each successive bill. Where we had been in the average income group, now we were poor and it was a struggle to keep up the payments on the car. Joy's needs had to come off the top and if we had a balance at the end of the month we bought clothes for Jonathan. After we had to reject several requests for new toys, he rarely asked again.

Jerry and I were bitter about a society which provided so little for families of moderate means. Indigent parents received aid and wealthy people had a choice of luxurious institutions for their handicapped children. But we nevertheless felt fortunate in having found a home which was only a two days' drive from home and less costly than most.

The months of Joy's residence at the "boarding school" both dragged and flew. Nothing was absolute. Life "as usual" was at best a sham. It would have been easier for me to yield to temptation and become a recluse than to force a smile and attend church and school meetings. But Jonathan had rights, too!

Every letter I wrote required careful preparation,

with no mention of happy family activities, meals which contained her favorite dishes, parties or social gatherings of her former classmates or neighbors, sickness, or death. No letter was written spontaneously and many times it took an hour or so to write a couple of paragraphs. She received a letter each week, except for the weeks we visited her.

Those monthly trips were expensive necessities. Joy invariably cried as we hugged and kissed her upon arrival. She enjoyed spending the night in a motel and eating in restaurants or having picnics, and seemed to have a good time no matter what we did for entertainment.

But when it was time to leave her, Joy didn't even seem to notice our departure or care. The excitement of the visit was over and her interest was now centered on telling the other girls what she had done, where she had stayed, and what she had eaten. Had she clung to us and cried, driving away without her would have been unbearable.

I remember one occasion in which it was impossible for Jerry to take time from his job. I flew alone to spend a couple of days with Joy. The first night as we were preparing for bed Joy suddenly began to cry noisily and bitterly. At first she refused to tell me what was bothering her. Then she said that the math teacher had put her in the sixth grade class and that they had also put her in a fifth grade reading class. I was shocked but Joy was chagrined.

She asked why she had been demoted, but I had no answer. Nor did I have a ready reply when she asked, "Mother, am I retarded?"

When I recovered my composure I told her that the

doctors who had tested her said she was not retarded. "Then why am I here? Everybody else is retarded."

She sat on my lap and I cuddled her, explaining that we had felt the boarding school would be better for her as classes were smaller and there was less competition. The explanation was not exactly a lie. It was more the truth with a heavy coat of varnish.

"Mother. The kids at home call me all sorts of names and say I'm an oddball. What's wrong with me? Why am I different?"

"Everyone is different, Honey. You're *my* girl, Daddy's girl, and Jonathan's sister. You are *our* special little sweetheart. God sent you to us to love and care for. The four of us are the Jennings family. That's where all of us are different, not only you!"

She kissed me with a noisy and wet smack. "Mommy, you're sweet, and I love you. When I get married I'm going to have six boys and six girls and I'll name every one of them Jerry and Jane so they'll be like you and Daddy!"

The "Mommy" did not go unnoticed, and I swallowed hard. It seemed wise to change the subject, and she answered the questions about meals and recreation at the school. Then she volunteered the information that she liked the girls in the dormitory but added, "Julie is fifteen and she has a second grade reading book. Lots of the kids can't count to ten or write their names. They're retards." With that, she began to cry again and begged to be taken home. "What's wrong with *me*?"

"You are *not* retarded, Sweetie. And I can't take you home. You don't have a plane ticket and I'm out of money to buy one. Remember what fun you had at the party and how you liked wearing the formal? And during the summer you'll have a swimming pool right outside with lots of girls to keep you company. At home there aren't many girls to play with, remember?"

I bit my tongue angrily. How stupid it was to have raked up unpleasant memories! Joy did not reply, obviously recalling life at home. Her eyes assumed their absent, glazed look; and we were poles apart. She said nothing more about her academic situation, her mentality, or returning home throughout the remainder of my visit. And, true to her pattern, she was more interested in seeing her friends again than in bidding me farewell.

Joy's relocation did not seem to be benefiting her, but no alternative was apparent. A second year at the home-school was impossible and inadvisable. Still we could not return Joy to the former public school classrooms. We suspected that her removal from town had been the subject of considerable discussion and conjecture. The teachers had assured me that they would not reveal the knowledge or details of Joy's examination and entry into the special school, but human nature being what it is we were not sure that Joy would not be subjected to ridicule or taunting should she return to the small town.

We were still in a forest.

The prospects seemed no better the second time we screened the directory, and the future loomed unpromising. As a last resort we began looking into the public school facilities of some of the larger cities that had special education classes available. They had not been recommended, but specialized classes appeared to be no worse than private schools for exceptional children. Our choices narrowed to a school of some kind, private tutoring, or keeping Joy at home all day with me and television.

We visited a number of schools and finally located one that sounded promising. Jerry conferred with his company's manager and arranged for a transfer. We put the house up for sale. Joy would be able to attend special classes at no extra cost to us and live at home. Jerry's worries would be lessened; and ends might meet for a change. It would be a relief to live normally and shed the shield of our white-lie-life in a small town.

Joy's return meant that Jonathan would have to make yet another adjustment. He had benefited by the separation. My time would again have to be split unevenly between them.

I had relaxed somewhat during the time Joy's physical well-being was not my sole responsibility. Jerry and I had quarreled less as tensions eased, and we hoped and prayed that the good points of our becoming a foursome again would balance the inevitable disadvantages. It was doubtful that the new city, home, neighbors and school would include a social life and companionship for Joy.

During her absence the seasons had made a complete cycle. Trees had spread their leafy umbrellas and then turned to red, orange, yellow and brown beauties before converting to bare skeletons. Flowers had bloomed, withered and died. Snow had blanketed the countryside, and it was time again for flowering trees and shrubs to glow in pastel or bright elegance.

As we drove to the school-home, dust devils swirled over newly-plowed fields and a faint touch of green in other fields hinted of an early crop. A few geese were already heading home, honking the good news of spring. God's pattern of life continued right on schedule.

We packed Joy's belongings into the car and began the return trip. Joy was anxious to see the new house and live with us again; her animation was brief, however. She slept most of the trip, and was primarily interested in eating. There was no apparent change in her personality.

She perked up briefly when we described her new room and told her that we had found a church near the new house. It had an active youth program and a junior choir, which meant she could attend social functions with a group occasionally. I had met with the young couple who directed youth activities and told them the true situation. It seemed better to do so before enrolling Joy in the group and then having to furnish explanations. My foolish pride was lessening. They empathized with us and assured me of their interest. They were wonderful Christians!

The first social gathering at the church was a picnic, much to Joy's delight. Food, we discovered, was an obsession with her. Her weight would continue to increase as she snacked on cereal, nuts, crackers, raisins, leftovers or anything she could find in the cupboard, refrigerator or freezer. She even ate unbaked canned biscuits!

The school's cafeteria was of prime interest as Joy entered the new facility. But it waned quickly. The novelty of her new clothes also wore off rapidly. She was reoccupying the rut she had left a year before. Joy preferred to sit and watch TV and balked at helping with housework or going to school. All of us were relieved when the school year ended, soon after Joy's return. Three months without a single parent-teacher conference!

Summer vacation presented fewer problems since schedules and routines could be ignored. When the principal contacted us prior to the resumption of classes in

September, Jerry and I felt betrayed. The school would not be able to take Joy again as it was abolishing the specialized training program and nothing would be available to suit Joy's needs.

We spent the balance of the summer contacting other schools, both private and public, and were elated when one school agreed to take her on a tuition basis. Once more we shopped for supplies, being careful to buy only items which were easily identifiable. The Special Education Department had its own block of lockers which would narrow the possibility of her losing her possessions.

Joy never mentioned the boys and girls in her classes or quizzed us about her mentality. She was, however, somewhat hesitant at having us visit her class and meet the teacher after the initial orientation. She shared the room with three hyperactive youngsters, a hydrocephalic boy, one nearly blind girl, two cerebral palsied children strapped into wheel chairs, a Mongoloid, and one whose handicap was no more obvious than Joy's. She introduced me to each student and later told me the nature of each child's affliction. None was a "borderline." I wondered if they had questioned Joy about her problem and what she had told them.

She was indifferent about school and said little about what transpired in the classroom. Pressure was minimal, homework assignments rare, accomplishments invisible.

It was not surprising, therefore, when Joy's teacher called us to arrange a conference. She was bored with the simpler classes and her borderline status made it difficult to gear the teaching to her greater capabilities. The teacher recommended private schooling with "resources adequate to meet her needs." We were given a month to relocate our daughter. She was "too smart" for special education but not smart enough for regular classes.

The available private schools flatly refused to enroll Joy. Their facilities were for college-bound youngsters, mostly of wealthy parents. The schools for handicapped children were very specialized and none fit her borderline needs. She was too old, not crippled, blind, deaf, emotionally disturbed, aphasic, cerebral palsied or epileptic. Public assistance agencies were suggested and we contacted each, one at a time. Their stock answer soon became a hateful broken record, "You do have a problem, Mrs. Jennings, and I wish we could help. Have you tried. . . ?"

It seemed inconceivable that we could not locate information about other borderlines. They have no totally unique handicap, and we knew there must be many like Joy. Someone, somewhere had the identical affliction, but none of the agencies could supply resource services to fit her category.

One social worker finally suggested we investigate the facilities of a small nearby school district. Success! Joy was admitted as a student in a special category, neither regular nor handicapped. Structured classes were especially set up to meet the needs of in-betweens. It sounded ideal. Following the school's suggestion, we decided to let Joy ride the bus part way to encourage her self-reliance.

Getting her to the bus stop on time five mornings each week was far from easy. But waiting for her arrival after school each afternoon was worse. Many days the bus arrived without her, as Joy dawdled at school the same as many years before. On a number of occasions she trusted people simply and blindly and could have been harmed, but the good Lord above must have been protecting her.

After three consecutive days of nail biting at the bus stop, Jerry and I agreed it might be better to drive her to and from school and dispense with public transportation, especially in bad weather. Jonathan had his house key and could walk the mile to his school, or perhaps ride with a neighbor now and then.

Jonathan seemed to understand. A year or so later he asked me about Joy's condition. He nodded seriously at my explanation that Joy needed special care and help in making decisions. Then he said, "The kids in the neighborhood call her a 'retard.' Is that what's the problem? Is she retarded?"

"No. She is just a little different from most girls."

He said nothing for quite some time and then asked a question which had haunted me many years. "If I get married some day, will my children be like her?"

I hugged him tightly and assured him that all children are individuals and that his children would be totally unaffected by any person except the parents, and that Joy's specific problems were not inherited or the fault of any one person. I wanted to avoid too much detail but I knew that too little would be just as confusing; I hoped and prayed that my explanation was adequate. How grateful I was he had not quizzed me a few years earlier when any reply would have been guesswork!

chapter 8

JOY ATTENDED the new school until she was seventeen, at which time the principal advised withdrawal. She had reached her limit. She could not concentrate long enough to gain any benefits from any course offered, even on a half-day schedule. In addition, she was a source of distraction to the others in the room. She wandered around the halls, spent much time in the rest rooms, went to the cafeteria kitchen to beg for snacks and feigned illness almost daily. She interrupted various music classes, asking to be included in the choral groups or just listen to instrumental instruction. The reactions of the other students—ridicule and open teasing usually—bewildered Joy. School was Disaster, Unlimited!

We had hoped Joy could graduate or receive a certificate of attendance for the full twelve years, since she placed so much importance on not being a dropout. Truthfully, we doubted she had actually learned much during her two years' matriculation program at the latest school; it had however kept her busy, and the regimen of a fixed schedule seemed beneficial.

The youth group at church afforded Joy her only social outlet. Each Sunday evening we drove her to the door and

127

then picked her up when the meeting adjourned. We avoided participation, hoping to make her less reliant on me especially, and us generally.

Most of the young people were kind, apparently recognizing her "differences," but no one knew how to cope with her bizarre actions and speech. She was included in the various outings and the weekly Sunday night supper-games-fellowship, but none of them went to her school and she had no contact of any kind with any of the group during the week. They were a captive group, and none would have chosen her for a companion.

Joy watched them graduate and leave for college, and a couple of the girls became engaged and then married. She duly noted their departure from the "high school" group. One day she asked me where she belonged. She was not in high school anymore nor was she in college. I told her that I thought she was welcome in any group she wished to attend, but I was not being honest with her. I had no idea where she fit in—in any segment of society.

Before long she lost interest in the Sunday evening meetings and ceased going to them. It had been her one social activity. Now she had none.

Jerry and I realized Joy might soon become a "vegetable" if left to her own devices. We wondered what type of employment would be suitable or available. She had no usable skills. The prospects of coping daily with her inertia and surliness and Jonathan's increasing tension and withdrawal grew into an insurmountable worry. I was totally inadequate to the task!

Once more we contacted the social agencies for help. "Sorry," head-shaking negative responses, and referrals to other sources were their stock result. Borderlines were neither fish nor fowl. They were misfits for whom no help was available. The agencies gave us sympathy and tissues for our tears—nothing more.

One referral was to a sheltered workshop, primarily geared to the limited capabilities of retarded people. We made the necessary arrangements for testing and interviews and Joy was told to report for work the next Monday.

I helped her dress and combed her hair so that she would make a better initial appearance and perhaps a better impression on the manager. She was alert and interested in her new job. She carried a sack lunch and chattered animatedly as she rode beside me.

At the end of the day she detailed her activities, described the workshop, the other employees and the manager, and told me how many items she had assembled. She talked all the way home, much to my surprise.

One day on the job was not enough to allow for much optimism, but her situation looked promising as she readied herself for work and then rode along the next morning. I had scarcely arrived home, however, when the manager telephoned, asking that I come for Joy. He had fired her the day before for refusing to follow instructions and she had become ugly and menacing when told to get back to work instead of typing a letter to some girls at her former school. Her disruptive actions ruled out any further attempts to employ her at the workshop.

Joy was waiting outside as I drove up, belligerent and confused, seeming not to understand that she could not work there any longer. "Why can't I?" There was no suitable answer to her question. At home, she settled herself in front of the television with a package of cookies and a bottle of pop.

The public agencies had been unable to help us in the past but we made the rounds again, repeating over and over Joy's history and our plight. It seemed a waste of time, but doing *anything* was better than *nothing*. One agency suggested occupational therapy to lengthen Joy's five-minute attention span.

This new approach sounded plausible, so we located a clinic in the older section of our city. True, it was in a deteriorating neighborhood but it was right at the bus stop. We were instructed to develop self-reliance. Joy must not rely on me or anyone else.

Riding the bus provided its full share of harrowing experiences. She frequently missed connections and lost her fare. I thanked God that she confided in me when she struck up a friendship with another regular passenger, a man about thirty. Joy announced she was going to marry him! She didn't know his name, but she would ask him the next day. It was back to driving her daily to and from her therapy sessions!

Joy was very fond of her therapist, a skilled young woman who took a personal interest in developing Joy's diverse skills. The several handcraft projects were attractive and useful, and Joy was proud of her achievements. After a year, her attention span had been expanded to thirty minutes, and supervised employment sounded possible if not probable.

The superintendent of a local convalescent-nursing home agreed to put Joy to work in the laundry room, at a minimal salary. His experience as a clinical psychologist would help Joy, who was similar to many of his former patients.

The job lasted three days. Joy preferred to visit the residents of the home and would not stick to her assigned work. The last straw was when she opened the medicine chest and helped herself to aspirins. Thank God it was *only* aspirin!

Our next employment effort was through our church. The minister thought she might be employed—without pay—in a domestic capacity at the retirement home. This meant living in a different town, in housing provided by the institution. The superintendent listened intently to our candid recitation of Joy's situation. His sympathetic attitude promised hope.

We hoped and prayed together that Joy's interest in church activities would motivate her and that she would find her niche. The elderly women residents would "mother" her and there would be no competition or pressure. Hopefully there would be no ridicule.

Joy's eyes shone as she went to invest in uniforms, envisioning herself as a nurse's aide. When we explained again that her duties would be primarily in the kitchen and not as a nursing attendant Joy shrugged and said that would be all right.

We drove to the retirement home, unpacked her belongings, and received instructions and a work schedule. Then I kissed her goodbye and left, afraid to hope that the man in charge could cope with our Joy.

Jerry, Jonathan and I ate our evening meal quietly. We were subconsciously listening for the phone to ring. The next day I did not leave the house, and began to relax when no call came from the home. Our spirits rose. And then they fell the following morning.

In only two days Joy had managed to set the kitchen

force and office staff in a tizzy. She flatly refused to do menial labor as assigned, would not get out of bed and report for work on time, wandered aimlessly around town and engaged in conversation with strangers. She got lost the second afternoon on one of her outings. While out she had stopped at a gas station to buy a can of pop, sat down to visit with the attendant, and decided to take up smoking. A vending machine supplied both cigarettes and matches, and the money in her purse was "to get rid of."

I still shiver as I recall the superintendent's comments regarding how he had located her and of the possible consequences of Joy's trusting nature, as well as the fire hazard of her smoking in her room. No ashtray was available so Joy had improvised. Her brand new compact served the purpose!

The superintendent suggested psychiatric counseling, as Joy seemed unable to understand the need to conform and seemed to be "away in space." She had threatened to "get" another employee in the kitchen, who claimed Joy intended to murder her. When we left the nursing home Joy was *nobody* and *nothing*. We needed divine guidance and help, for the possibility of schizophrenia seemed less remote. Joy's mental state was deplorable. Each rejection and frustration drove her farther and farther from normal.

"God, you've just got to help her, and help all of us," I cried out silently but passionately, recalling the way Joy had stuffed her soiled uniforms and possessions into the suitcase without saying a word. She had been angry and bewildered at having to leave, had cursed the other employees and her boss, and had thrown several new items into the wastebasket. Her violence, which was not unusual at home, was greater than before. I understood her co-worker's fear of physical harm.

Joy's large size and vicious temper, combined with a total lack of self-control or judgment, presented a frightening situation. I hoped she never saw through my bluff and realized that I, too, feared her anger.

Once we were on the highway heading home, Joy yawned noisily and promptly fell asleep. The new problem removed any optimism we might have had left. There was nothing more to try. There was no other place for her. Joy and her problems were solely my responsibility. The prospects terrified me.

Why, I wondered, was there no provision for helping borderlines in families with average incomes? Why had *we* been cursed with this problem? Life was not a series of peaks and valleys anymore—it was one endless chasm. Psychiatric help might be right for Joy, as the superintendent suggested; but such counseling might be of even more help to her mother.

As we neared the house, I roused Joy. I was startled to see her look at me with hatred and loathing.

"Why did you have to come and spoil things for me again? Every time I get a job you poke your nose in it and won't let me work. They liked me at the nursing home and the other one, too. You mean old woman! I hate you!"

Aghast, I said nothing. She began to cry, screaming several times, "I hate you!" I believed her and was terrified.

We took her things into the house wordlessly and she headed for the sofa and television. A cartoon caught her attention briefly, and then she prepared a snack.

God was now my only possible source of help. I prayed

again, although it frankly seemed he was not going to answer our pleas. Surely, I thought, he would not punish our Jonathan for my sins, whatever they might have been. But the Bible verse, "The sins of the fathers . . . ," kept crossing my mind. What had I done to deserve such cruel punishment? Or was it perhaps my parents who were to blame? Or Jerry? Or his parents? Finding a scapegoat somehow seemed all-important at the time.

I gulped another tranquilizer and struggled to act naturally at the dinner table that evening. Joy was in a happy mood and seemed to have forgotten the events of the day. She hummed and also sang her all-time favorite, "Jesus loves me, this I know, for the Bible tells me so." It never failed to rake up memories of her toddler days and it usually brought on a weeping session for me. Jesus might love Joy, but he obviously did not love *me*, I thought, mired as I was in self-pity.

Many times I eyed a narrow bridge which we crossed on the way to the grocery and shopping center. It might hold the answer, I thought. If I hit it head on, hard enough, surely neither Joy nor I could survive. I had to be certain that we would not live as cripples and be still more of a burden to Jerry and Jonathan. Joy and I together were dragging both of them down with us. Each day the bridge pulled me closer to suicide and murder, although I could not use those words even in thinking of the contemplated acts.

Each day that we neared the bridge, its magnet failed as memories of Jonathan and his needs kept me on the road. At twelve he was almost entirely self-reliant, as he had always been forced to be. I was a 100 percent failure as his mother, but I *did* prepare his meals and care for his clothes.

The temptation to hit the concrete railing was great, but not great enough. I was too cowardly to take that final step. Each day I hated myself more, doubted each act more, and edged closer to mental illness.

As I floundered and became more deeply mired in the quagmire of doubt, I became more convinced God had deserted us, and my prayers changed. "If you exist, God, but you won't help us, at least send us some sign. Show us where to find help. Show us what to do," I begged daily.

Wavering faith strengthened the temptation to skip church and stay at home with Joy, but enough of a remnant of belief in a loving God prompted me to attend as part of the family group. Sermons seemed filled with hidden messages for me, and I listened intently for the minister's innuendos. Infant baptisms were painful ordeals and I could not bear to see a pregnant woman, wondering if *her* baby would be handicapped. Normal children were comparison points with Joy.

I made no pretense of understanding my child, but Jerry was adamant in his belief that we would find a solution to our quandary if we kept looking hard enough and long enough. His attitude perplexed me and caused more quarrels. I doubted his love for me, and actually decided to run away from the dilemma. Let *him* handle the kids and their ever-increasing squabbles. *Then* he would understand!

I packed a few things and drove off. But God had other plans for me. A truck sideswiped my car, ran me into the ditch, smashed the trunk and ruined the suitcase filled with my belongings. The accident should have been fatal for me, but I walked away from it. Jerry came for me after my car was towed away, and I returned to the constant strife. I was a failure even at running away!

My bruises and concussion healed before long, and life continued to rock along as before, except that Jerry arranged to spend more time with both children and relieve me of some responsibility. I withdrew my suit for divorce when he convinced me I was not all the way liable for Joy's handicap, as I had come to believe. "We can make it together, some way, Janey. Neither of us can do it alone."

His level head and judgment saved our marriage, and I rejoice!

Joy occasionally meandered throughout the neighborhood and seemed to watch for times when I could not physically restrain her. I became her jailer, she mine. It was not even safe to leave the two children by themselves, for Jonathan could not cope with her behavior. A time or two we found sitters "for our son," but Joy's threats of injury and verbal abuse made us abandon any future outings without her along.

Jonathan now begged to stay home rather than be subjected to the embarrassment of Joy's erratic actions. He became more and more withdrawn and would not discuss the situation with Jerry or me. I know now that the black eye he got was probably caused by a fight that resulted from taunts from other boys in the neighborhood. I can only guess at what went on, for he has never told me. Nor did I learn until many years later that he preferred to stay alone, terrified of creaks and doors that rattled when the wind blew strongly, and huddled near the back door in the dark, rather than accompany us on visits to her after we found a home for her.

Jonathan's schoolwork also became a source of worry to us. His report cards reflected nothing of his proven high intelligence and his teachers said he refused any challenge. Competitive sports did not interest him either. Jerry and I accepted the blame for his attitudes.

Since we had been unable to goad Joy into better schoolwork or demand higher achievements, we felt it unfair to expect Jonathan to produce more than he did. We also found it hard to chide him when he performed below his capabilities, since we accepted Joy's accomplishments, whatever they were.

Jonathan bore his heavy burden silently, and his hurts deepened with each year. He seemed old beyond his age. After one particularly bad report card, he revealed the fears that gnawed at his mind. "Mother, am I like Joy? The kids call her a retard and make nasty cracks about her all the time. I wonder if they think that about me, too."

"No, son, no! You know you have no problems like Joy's. We don't know why she is handicapped, but she is slightly. But you are perfectly normal!" I hugged his rigid little body tightly, hoping to calm his deep fears. "Joy is different. Period."

Joy definitely was different. She was a young adult chronologically but a child in every action. She refused to get out of bed until nearly noon, and then ate breakfast in her night clothes while watching soap operas or cartoons or joining in the game shows. At noon she demanded lunch, regardless of when she had finished breakfast. She would not make her bed or dress, and frequently she decided to visit a neighbor—barefooted and in her pajamas—if she could sneak out while I was busy and unable to monitor her actions. She would neither bathe nor brush her teeth. Her hair was a constant smelly tangle. She seemed resigned to doing nothing. Occasionally she put together a few pieces of a jigsaw puzzle or played the piano. Sometimes she played jacks by herself or shuffled a deck of cards for a game of solitaire which she always "won." She conversed with "She" daily. She was bored, bewildered and totally frustrated.

I could not motivate Joy. If I insisted she do something not to her liking, she cursed and swore or threatened to kill me. She seemed fascinated by the word "kill." Several times as she stood at the top of the stairway swinging Jonathan's baseball bat or waving a carving knife in the kitchen, her anger was sufficiently intense to have driven her to murder. I knew she must never suspect the depth of my fear of her. I knew, too, that outside help was our only hope.

Our family physician recommended psychiatry, believing schizophrenia was a possibility. Eventually we agreed to consultations. Private therapists were booked far ahead, but the only alternative was three to six weeks' residence at the state mental hospital. We could not bring ourselves to placing her behind bars and chose to wait the three months until a psychiatrist could see Joy. Ninety days! I didn't think I could make it.

Many times I hated Joy and simultaneously detested myself. I knew she could not control her actions and that the whirlpool of frustration was sucking her down, down, down. How deep her bafflement went, I'll never know. No one will ever know if Joy's swallowing twelve child-strength aspirins was a suicide attempt or merely an effort to stop a headache. I found the empty bottle a few hours after she took the pills and my scalp tingled, pondering her next such act.

We had experimented with each new medication as it was made available and investigated the possibility of repatterning her damaged brain, but neither suited Joy. We could not wait for the local psychiatrist. Our last fragment of pride dwindled and we at last decided to apply for a complete psychiatric examination—and commitment—at the state hospital.

Once more we packed Joy's suitcase. She was animated at the prospect of taking a trip as a break in her ordinary routine, but asked no questions about the destination. Jonathan stayed home.

As we were answering stock questions Joy suddenly grasped the situation, and tears rolled down her cheeks. She said in a dull, flat, lifeless voice, "But I'm not mentally ill."

We told her she was there to have some tests run because she was so tense and nervous. The supply of answers was depleted. "But Mommy, I'm not mentally ill!" she sobbed as an attendant came to accompany her down the stark, barren hall. She looked beaten, but she did not look back to see both of us in tears.

Joy could have two visitors a week. She would be kept in a locked area. Beyond that information I dared not think. "God help us if this is the worst mistake we've made so far!"

I went alone for the first visit, a horrendous ordeal. Joy looked sloppier than she ever had at home—her ripped clothes unmended, and her natural lethargy in-

creased by tranquilizers. After her happy-to-see-you
greeting and hug, Joy said little. She was not especially
interested in learning about our activities and talked list-
lessly about a dance she had attended at the recreation
hall. She said she had written letters to former friends
and acquaintances and neighbors, but said nothing about
what she told them. No one mentioned a letter from her.
She wrote none to us.

A conference with the chief psychiatrist was scheduled
for three weeks after her commitment. Jerry and I found
the wait excruciatingly long and difficult. We doubted we
had done the right thing in placing her in the hospital for
tests.

It was a great relief to learn the tests had proved Joy
was *not* schizophrenic, but highly tense and nervous.
Instead of running more tests for the full six-weeks
period, they felt it best to release her that day but gave us
no further recommendations. We took her home that
afternoon, perplexed at the prospects and equipped with
no guidelines for the future.

We rode in silence, engrossed in thought. Suddenly Joy
demanded to know why we had placed her in the loony
cage. "I'm *not* mentally ill! You knew that, you bastards!"
She yelled the words several times before quieting. Jerry
and I gasped in unison. He was stunned and speechless,
but I told her firmly not to talk to us that way ever again.

"Don't you like the way I talk? Well, I don't care, you
old bitch. Why don't you go to hell!"

"Joy!"

She yelled it again and again.

"Stop that this instant!" I screamed, and without

thinking slapped Joy across the face. She began to cry loudly and violently.

Soon her mood changed. She was contrite, her rage spent. "I'm sorry. I didn't mean it, Mother. Please forgive me. I don't know why I said that. I love you both so much."

"Just be sure you never again talk that way to me, young lady!"

"You won't forgive me? I said I was sorry." She waited a few seconds and then continued. "I'm *not* sorry, really, and I was lying. I hate you!" Her fury had returned. Then she cried once more, noisily and without letup.

That night I prayed a new prayer. "If you exist, God, send us hope. If there is no place at all where Joy can be happy, then take her, God. I don't have the courage to hit that bridge. The 'accident' might not be fatal. Please, God—if you really do exist and if you love any one of the four of us at all—please help Joy! Show us the way!"

chapter **9**

W<small>E</small> KNEW there was no alternative. Joy could not live at home in a normal society. Once more we read the directory for listings of homes where Joy could live a simple, uncomplicated life. Schooling was not an issue; her age and almost normal I.Q. were. Available homes for adults were scarce and most residences were for severely handicapped children. The most recent tests revealed regression and her I.Q. rating was 74, not low enough to qualify for residence in a state institution. From what we had read, a state institution was a last resort, and primarily an overcrowded place of stagnation for indigents. But in our frantic state of mind, we looked into *everything*.

We contacted several homes by letter, by telephone and in person, but without success. Each chaotic day seemed worse than the day before, and we walked an emotional tightrope with no safety net underneath.

In desperation I called Joy's former occupational therapist and social worker, both of whom I considered true friends who were earnest in their desire to help Joy. I told them I was at the end of the line and asked for suggestions on some course of action. There was nothing more I could do or try.

"Have you thought of church-sponsored homes, Jane?" the social worker asked.

I told her of having explored that possibility and reminded her of the attempt at employment in a retirement-nursing home operated by our denomination. Our church had no home for handicapped young people of any type.

"Lots of church homes for handicapped people make no distinction as to denomination. Some give preference to their own members but there is no hard and fast rule that they will not or cannot take in others. Think about it and maybe you'll find your answer."

The possibility sounded reasonable and I assured her that my next step would be to reread the directory for likely prospects.

Ten minutes later she phoned again. "Jane, I was just going over the morning's mail and I found a letter and brochure from a brand-new home which sounds ideal. I can't tell whether it fits Joy's case exactly, but it is only 150 miles away. You might want to call them and set up an appointment for an interview and inspection."

"It sounds too good to be true," I replied with weighted hope as she detailed the facilities and requirements for residence. Three days later I drove to the home for the initial contact while Jerry stayed home from work to supervise Joy's activities.

The minister in charge of the modern, beautiful institution was genuinely concerned and he generated optimism mixed with pessimism. Joy was over the top age limit and the goal of the home was to teach fundamental reading and writing and basic skills for limited employment. Almost every child enrolled in the school was se-

verely retarded or physically impaired. The parents had
each paid a $10,000 enrollment fee and were paying
monthly room and board, and tuition charges as well.

My spark of hope died. This visit, like the others,
appeared to be a total waste of time and wear and tear on
the car.

Then he said, "Mrs. Jennings, if you can make yourself
accept less than ideal surroundings and accept the fact
that your child is not ever going to be normal, there is
another home operated by our church which may take her.
It is only for girls and women, and it has no age limit. It's
about a hundred miles farther from your home. They care
for all kinds of handicapped females in a self-help arrangement. The ones who are more capable help the less
fortunate or more severely handicapped. It gives them a
sense of personal worth and self-esteem."

I was afraid to hope again, but this suggestion seemed
to be better than all the others we had eliminated in our
search. I could not stop the tears as I listened to his
description of the home. He volunteered to telephone the
minister-superintendent of the related home and set up an
appointment for the following weekend. We would arrange
to have all of Joy's medical and school records sent for
their review. We didn't even mention cost. Somehow we
would manage if it was a suitable haven for Joy.

Joy's higher-than-some I.Q. rating was not stressed.
Would it make her ineligible? It seemed ironic that we had
once been so proud of her having been classified as not
retarded. Many attitudes had changed over the years.

Now "institutionalization" was only an eight-syllable
word; "retardation" a four-syllable condition which we still
felt stigmatic; "brain damage" only a physical condition;

and "never" much too long a time.

Another major change in our reaction to Joy's handicapped state was that we could dump the entire situation
on a stranger's desk for clinical analysis and dissection.
Each facet of her condition could be studied in a sterile,
test-tube manner. I still had not recognized that I had to
give the problem back to God and stop trying to handle
things myself.

I was expecting God to perform miracles, and I was
demanding too much of Joy. I know that now, but I did not
then. While I had recited the Lord's Prayer all my life, I
had never really thought about the words, ". . . *thy* will be
done. . . ." *His* will, not mine. Surely he was the one who
was now guiding us to the home recommended by the
minister-superintendent.

The large red brick building at the top of a winding
driveway resembled a hospital, but the reception room
had none of its sterile atmosphere. A small Mongoloid
woman was mopping the recessed area, and another was
busy arranging flowers in a vase. A beautiful girl of about
fifteen, with no apparent handicap, was visiting with the
receptionist. A large painting of Jesus Christ surrounded
by little children hung over the door. The bulletin board
was covered with childish colored and painted pictures.

Joy's eyes missed nothing. Her neatly brushed hair (for
a change) and well-fitting new skirt and blouse looked
slightly out of place, but her actions were similar to those
of the girls and women we saw as we followed the superintendent through the dormitories, kitchen, recreation
hall, laundry and hospital section.

I tried to visualize Joy as a resident. What type of
work would she do, or could anyone succeed in making her

work? She liked to work with food, but only if she could nibble as she worked and gobble if she so desired. And she was determined to do things her own way.

How would Joy fit in with the other residents? Would she be accepted and have friends and companions? Would *she* accept *them*? I wondered if she was mentally comparing herself with the girls she saw, many of whom were horribly misshapen and deformed. She might be a misfit here, too, more an unhappy probability in view of her relatively normal appearance. How long had the others been here and how had the parents of the girls managed the separation and financing?

Some were playing games or cards, others worked puzzles or watched television. Some rocked incessantly in their chairs and a few sat in wheelchairs, arms flailing and heads jerking. A large, gray-haired resident slumped in her chair, drooling and making odd grunting sounds as she struggled to remove the belt that held her upright. I reeled, but Joy made no sign of revulsion.

She was interested in the manually powered laundry equipment and the indoor drying lines filled with bed linens and diapers. The bright quilts and spreads were like those we had seen in the private and semi-private rooms and in the wards where eight to ten girls slept.

If Joy were accepted here, would she be housed in a ward with many others or in a private room? The multiple occupancy seemed less than desirable, and I could not envision Joy in that situation. The cuddle toys and dolls resting on pillows seemed perfectly normal, although most of the small girls were housed in a separate wing, as were the old, old women. The "girls" in this ward were in their thirties, forties, fifties. . . .

I avoided any comparison with Joy's bright and pretty room at home, and said to Jerry, "It's certainly no finishing school, but she wouldn't fit into one of those anyway. It *is* clean and smells nice, and it's functional." He nodded.

"Our girls work up to their capacities, without too much pressure and *no* competition. They like to feel needed and worthwhile. Many of them have blossomed just because they are able to help someone less fortunate.

"We have no classrooms and are able to keep costs down that way. Also our church makes large contributions to help maintain this home and similar facilities for boys. It's plain but frills aren't important to our residents."

I glanced at Joy, standing across the room where a group of three girls were dusting and cleaning a bookcase. She always acted as if frills were *very* important. She might be the exception to the rule. Yet she had never selected her own clothes or room furnishings and had always left such choices up to me.

It seemed uncanny that the superintendent had anticipated our questions; that made the inspection-interview easier. He suggested that Joy wait in the handcraft room and watch the girls engaged in various activities while we discussed our business in his office.

"If you decide to leave Joy here in our care, there are certain things we must talk about now. If you have any doubts, there will be time to look into those areas, for we have no opening now. Joy will be on a waiting list if you wish, but we have no way of guessing when an individual may be accepted or what type of housing will be available."

His candor was a welcome change from the everything-will-be-just-wonderful description we had received at a couple of other places which would have been far from wonderful.

His first question was, "How long do you anticipate leaving Joy?" Neither of us could answer. We both accepted the fact that Joy could not live happily at home and that her presence there was more or less intolerable. Her frustration was too great and her behavior too dangerous some of the time. We could not say yes when he asked if we wanted lifetime custodial care. If she was miserably unhappy or we could not scrape up the monthly fee, we would have to look for some other home-away-from-home. The cost, he said, would depend on the available space and could not be set in advance.

The directory had cited a very low monthly rate, which had cast doubts in my mind as to the desirability of the home. It was the minimum and applicable to multiple occupancy, the superintendent explained. "Our rates are much lower than most. Our members and our national church board contribute to our upkeep."

He then asked us Joy's I.Q. rating. The application form specifically stated that the home was for mentally retarded females, but Joy was a borderline. The status seemed less limiting and I could not dub her a retardate. "It varies from 74 to 103 depending on how her central nervous system is working when she is being tested," Jerry replied.

I looked at him and wondered if Joy would be rejected because of her nearly normal mentality. This home offered what others had not, a chance for Joy to find herself in helping others and using her talents to advantage.

Many questions remained to be answered. Both Jerry and I faltered when we came to the space on the form that pertained to a would-be resident's sexual experience. It seemed off-key and we wondered why they asked such a question. The superintendent noticed our reaction and pushed the box of tissues in my direction. It seemed as if every time I had been conferring with a teacher, doctor, counselor or psychologist a box of tissues was handy. They expected emotional parents!

I assured him that to my knowledge Joy had had no sexual experience. He explained that many brain-damaged girls whose sense of judgment is impaired have had extensive activity and that some have had babies. "They live in a misty, half-world of unreality at home. Any casual invitation is considered an order. Small tokens of affection are immediately 'clothed in wedding gowns,' according to the parents of one of our girls. It is not at all uncommon for these innocent girls to be raped with their consent." I reached for a second tissue.

"Some of them are oversexed and would be a problem here, in spite of our caring for females only. We do have male maintenance people and some of the girls try to run away at times. We don't keep them if they are troublemakers."

His words were alarming. I recalled Joy's acquaintance with the gas station attendant and the man on the bus whom she had planned to marry. I also thought of her intended six boys and six girls and her formal wedding plans.

"It's important that you have a pretty good idea of our operation if Joy comes to live with us. Our girls are treated the same, no matter what their background. Some are nearly normal and others need constant care. A few come from well-to-do families, but most are daughters of working people. Some have no families left.

"One, Martha, is eighty-three. She makes quite a bit of money selling her paintings, but she can't read or write. Lucille is a little younger than Martha, and she plays the piano and sings in the choir. She has a perfect pitch and it thrills me to hear her singing lullabies to her doll. Neither of them has a living relative."

He had answered two unasked questions. What would happen to Joy if Jerry and I did not outlive her? and were there facilities for music? His next remark piqued my interest. "Some of our brighter residents primp and daub makeup on their faces but most of them don't care about niceties for the most part. They are easygoing, happy-go-lucky. They set their own pace here." He had twice mentioned "brighter residents" and "nearly normal residents." I wondered if they might also be borderlines.

We were out of questions and he had no more points to cover. Our inspection convinced us that Joy would be safe from fire or severe weather. A full-time nurse and nearby hospital reassured us of medical care if an emergency arose. Routine immunizations ruled out epidemics of ordinary diseases, and they were a standard requirement. A certificate from the State Licensing Board assured us that this home met the standards for safe operation.

We had many assurances—but none which guaranteed kindness, comfort and companionship.

This home was different from all the others we had visited and contacted, however. I admit we had not inspected any other church home, so any comparison in that category was impossible. I asked if Joy would be expected to change her denomination. "We have all faiths represented here. Protestant, Catholic, Jewish. But we have only one church."

"Church has always been important to Joy and she enjoys singing in the choir. She probably would like to join it here."

"That's up to her. Anyone who wants to sing in robes up front is welcome to join. The more the merrier."

We felt this home held promise, but were glad no decision was necessary at the moment. We would have to think about it before placing her there for the rest of her life.

The inspection-interview was over and we returned to the craft room to pick up our daughter. We heard the familiar song as we neared the door. Joy was playing and singing, "Yes, Jesus loves me. Yes, Jesus loves me. Yes, Jesus loves me. The Bible tells me so."

I grabbed for Jerry's hand. Perhaps Jesus would help in making our decision. And perhaps Joy would discard her imaginary companion. She might have a real friend to walk and talk with. Joy had first walked alone at seventeen months, then she has walked alone for nineteen years. She needed a companion.

It was easy to be wooed by optimism. But the "school of experience" had taught us skepticism instead of hope. I crossed off each twenty-four hours, month by month, watching the mail in hopes of being notified of an opening at the home. We lived in limbo as our litany of worries increased and Joy's behavior noticeably regressed.

We thought of hunting for another church-sponsored home. We might have no chance of an opening for years in the one we had visited! Our first impressions had not been too favorable because of the white-uniformed personnel and the absence of a "homey" atmosphere. What if things did not work out there?

We wondered if perhaps we should look for temporary placement. No arrangement was going to be gold-plated or even gilded with mica. Back and forth we wobbled, unsure of our every proposal.

Habit had forced me to listen to the minister of our church, and one Sunday his words suddenly jolted me upright.

"It is a fallacy that affliction always results from evil. It is simply untrue that bad things happen only to bad people or that good things happen only to good people. Violent deaths and family tragedies are not necessarily due to sin. Still an inbred and inflexible morality somehow makes us connect pain and trouble with wrongdoing. No person dares base any judgment solely on outward appearances. C.S. Lewis once said, 'God whispers to us in our pleasures; he speaks to us in our consciences; but he shouts to us in our pain.'"

The pastor had not blamed the "sins of the fathers." Why?

I was still mulling the Lewis quotation over in my mind when the pastor said, "Everyone needs a sense of being in a loving community as a reason to live. A detached person, unaccepted anywhere, is cut loose from the moorings of civilization. A sense of belonging is what gave the early Christians a pungent vitality and saved the world from paganism."

The minister was talking about *Joy*! And he was relaying God's message to *me*!

The timing of the sermon was, I believe, divinely inspired. It sent me back to my knees. "Dear God. I can't handle this. You can. Do it your way. Amen."

When the congregation recited the Lord's Prayer in unison every word had a special meaning for me. Joy must have listened to the sermon too, for she held my hand tightly as we sang the morning hymn, "What a Friend We Have in Jesus."

That Sunday's service was a much needed stimulant for my spiritual paralysis. I somehow knew then that God would soon bring us help. It was no great surprise therefore when a letter arrived the next day advising us that a semi-private room would be available in two weeks! Tears of joy came to my eyes! The higher cost was still less than quoted by any other home we had contacted, and no extra clothing or linens were required. A letter would take too long, so I telephoned the superintendent immediately to reserve the room before he changed his mind and accepted some other girl.

The next fourteen days were filled with excitement. Joy paid little attention to the readying of her clothes, the packing or the preparations, however. We were a bit wary as we once again left the house in a steady downpour.

This trip was different from previous ventures. The inclement weather did not worry me excessively, and Joy did not sleep the entire time. She sang along with the radio and was unusually pleasant and animated, eager to arrive at her new home-away-from-home.

The rain had stopped before we arrived, and the sun was shining brightly. Joy methodically dodged the puddles instead of stepping in each one, and scurried to the front door. A smiling Mongoloid adult-child stood in the hall near the superintendent's office. She dropped her doll, and Joy bent to retrieve it. The small woman reached to hug her and Joy returned the embrace.

It seemed fortuitous that this was one of Joy's better days. We so wanted her to make a good impression on the superintendent. She was engrossed in admiring the doll and inspecting the office and its furnishings. When the superintendent suggested that Joy might like to go to the recreation room, she agreed, kissed us goodbye, and then walked with her newfound friend, arm in arm, seemingly happy to have a companion. The woman's obvious handicap did not bother Joy at all; it would not rub off onto her!

She had never been with us in spirit, but that day she left our presence. She was twenty.

Today Joy is thirty-four. Realization that God had answered our prayers did not come as a dramatic bolt of enlightenment as Joy walked down the hall and into her new way of life. It was a slow process.

At first Joy resented the rigid discipline and the regulations of the home and the unaccustomed give-and-take involved in sharing a bedroom. She did her assigned jobs half-heartedly and sloppily, and sometimes rebelled and refused to do anything at all as she had done at home. Her independence made the regimented existence chafe, and her frequent outbursts of temper, disobedience and profane tongue-lashings resulted in punishment in the form of being grounded.

She did not learn from one experience to the next and was grounded over and over again for unacceptable behavior. Each time she told us, "I got what I deserved." The incident with the ashtray when she was a tiny tot always flashed across my memory as she related her troubles. I dreaded the possibility of her being sent home as an undesirable resident who could not be tamed.

Her absence afforded me time to read books and
magazine articles. I searched like a prospector for similar
experiences to my own. I wept for the little girls of Dale
Evans Rogers and Pearl Buck, the Kennedys' Rosemary
and the Humphreys' granddaughter. I silently thanked
visually limited Anne Sullivan Macy for her advice to
"treat a handicap as an opportunity for courage" when
writing about Helen Keller. I felt a sense of camaraderie
with cerebral palsied Karen Killilea's mother, who said
Karen was "born in the dark womb of ignorance," a
situation which determination and science are now cor-
recting. Two years ago I recognized Joy as I was studying
a textbook dealing with learning disabilities.

Occasionally I waste time pondering what life might
have been if.... But that is of no consequence now. We
placed Joy and we feel God sent us to that home. We took
it on trust. But as the years have passed, we have come to
know that the strangers to whom we gave Joy, her substitute parents, have provided the "life" we could not give
her. We could only give her an empty existence.

Knowing now that Joy is protected from others and
herself has helped us relax and feel comfortable in having
placed her in an institution. At first, however, we relin-
quished the parent role slowly. We did not like to take
orders affecting our visits or Joy's outings with us. When
Joy complained now and then of the food, we "made up for
it" by indulging her in expensive meals. We gave her too
many treats and bought her too many clothes and trin-
kets. They only served to cause jealousy among the other
girls, and meant little or nothing to Joy. She frequently
gave her new gifts to others after a day or so.

A couple of years after we had placed Joy in the home,

one of the attendants commented about Joy's higher-than-average I.Q. "She needs our help here more than the severely retarded patients who don't face competition and frustration. They aren't as aware of rejection and it doesn't bother them much. They could live at home if their parents could handle their physical needs, but most mothers aren't nurses or therapists."

I welcomed her understanding of what it's like to be a parent of a handicapped child, and secretly wondered if she too had a handicapped son or daughter. I believed her when she told me that she had a special feeling for Joy and loved her very dearly. She brightened the day which had begun drearily.

Joy's hair was more unkempt than usual, and her clothing was disheveled, soiled and not suited to the climate. I was embarrassed both by her appearance and her childish actions. I envied Jonathan who had begged to be left at home rather than endure a day with Joy on the children's playground equipment of the city park. It meant staying alone overnight, for he refused to visit his best friend again, unless something would come up to change his mind. He gave no reason. We reluctantly agreed; he had been her "babysitter" long enough. He had taken care of his own needs all of his life and at the age of fourteen would manage nicely by himself.

When we returned the next day, Jonathan assured us everything had gone smoothly with no problems. I did not doubt his word, but several years later I discovered he had not told us the whole truth. When the house had creaked and the door had rattled in the strong wind during the night, he had awakened and panicked. He then had crept downstairs and huddled by the back door, wrapped in a blanket, listening for some burglar or intruder who might harm him. When day broke, he had forced himself to make the rounds of the house, and then he had gone to bed and slept.

Jonathan lied because his hurts were too deep for him to fathom. All of us bear scars from the turbulent trauma, but his go deeper than ours. He preferred to stay alone and be terrified by the unknown rather than suffer through another day of steady embarrassment. I am frankly grateful he kept his secret and did not tell me the whole truth.

Several times since Joy left, I have tried to explain Joy's physical impairment to Jonathan, but he still does not want to know more. He too has built a shell against hurts, an armor which still closes them out—or keeps them in.

Self-doubts weighed heavily on both of our children. Our situation was not easy either. Joy's handicap necessitated our making her decisions for her, but Jonathan resented any help or instruction we offered. He may have regarded assistance as an indication of lack of confidence in him. Joy's rejection and frustration made her pull farther within herself, but Jonathan's pushed him farther from us. Our normal parental interest in his school work, his friends, his outside activities and his housing he regards as an invasion of his privacy. In essence he has become a stranger to the three of us.

Today he keeps his own counsel. He still visits us now and then. It makes us sad to realize that we know more about our neighbors' children than we do about our own son. We pray he will some day finish college and we can truly be a family again sometime. God has done such wondrous things for Joy and Jerry and me that I know he can also bless Jonathan and give him the bounty of his love and grace.

Occasionally I do wonder if Jonathan still has fears of having a defective child. He is twenty-eight and unmarried. The christening dress I made for Joy and our grandchildren and great-grandchildren ... it's in the plastic bag in the attic. The little white linen suit Jonathan wore for his christening is in another.

Once we were convinced that this was the place for Joy and that lifetime placement for her was right, we made suitable arrangements. We set up a trust fund with our life insurance as collateral to relieve Jonathan of any future financial burden. Personnel at the home will take care of Joy's physical requirements, and the minister and church activities will provide for her spiritual needs. She socializes with many of the other residents.

Noticeable improvement in Joy's behavior, personality and appearance came about some four years ago when the home expanded and Joy moved into the new space. She delighted in showing us her neat and clean private room with its colorful new furnishings—which *she* maintained. We agreed that the extra cost was justifiable.

She also serves as a teacher's aide and she thrills when one of the less capable girls masters a few new words or number combinations under her tutelage. Joy herself resumed her interrupted schooling under the basic education plan for adults. It was a king-size moment for all of us when Joy "graduated," complete with cap and gown. The light in her eyes outshone the flashbulbs as Jerry photographed the momentous occasion! She was beautiful and radiant.

Her appearance matters now, and she sometimes

wears a small amount of makeup. She bathes daily and
shampoos her hair several times weekly. She picks at
herself now and then but rarely tears her clothing, which
she selects and pays for from her earnings.

Joy's more mature appearance does not fit her occasional childish reactions. A fly or other insect in the car
causes near panic, but a summer evening's cricket concert
accompanied by the flashing lights of a ladybug keep her
animated and happy. The whir of a hummingbird's wings
fascinates Joy. Her favorite birds are still the gaudier
cardinals, blue jays and scarlet-topped woodpeckers. The
antics of squirrels amuse her almost as much now as in her
childhood. She laughs and enjoys watching them chase
each other across telephone lines or dart from tree branch
to tree top in a game of tag, their mouths carrying nesting
materials or an installment on the winter food supply.

Joy hangs back as we pass a department store's Santa
Claus, and might stop if we were not with her. She plays
jacks and hopscotch, draws childlike pictures with her
crayons and cannot stay within the lines of a coloring
book, does needlepoint and knits intricate pattern stitches
perfectly, plays the piano and chord organ, sings in the
choir, and enjoys the swimming pool, outings to the zoo,
picnics, parties, concerts and the opera. Holiday celebra-
tions are gala events in her life, especially Halloween
costume parties and the Easter egg hunts which she
interprets as related to her birthday.

The wide span of social activities, so important to her
progress, could never be duplicated elsewhere in a so-
called normal setting. This aspect of the home-away-
from-home was not offered at the time we placed Joy and,
to us, is the frosting on the cake. We view the home not as

a placebo but as a source of long-range comfort for all four of us.

Joy's fundamental needs for companionship and something to do have been met, and she apparently has come to terms with herself. Being needed, inclusion instead of rejection, and enjoyment of diverse activities have all figured in effecting wondrous changes in her personality. She has gradually become less tense and antagonistic and more cooperative. She takes disappointments stoically instead of bellicosely. The tigress of a decade ago is a sweet, tractable young lady today.

Today, on her thirty-fourth birthday, it is difficult to reconcile our happy Joy with the uncontrollable Joy of those bad days. Her workshop boss and Joy are good friends. Quotas are important, and Joy is upset if she fails to complete her share of the assignments. Her paltry salary is big money that she earned! Her above-average manual skills are put to use helping the less capable co-workers. Joy is proud of herself and is *somebody*.

She is proud that she is *not* a dropout and that she has a job. She has self-respect. The stigma of being "different" does not seem to bother her now that she is in her own element and not in the penumbra of "normal" society.

Joy has never inquired about why she lives in the home. She uses the word "retarded" easily and frequently, but not in relation to herself. She is aware of the various afflictions of individual residents and I think this is a common subject for discussion among the girls.

Once she casually mentioned a group of brain-damaged girls who had gone to some program away from the home. She did not use the term "minimal brain dysfunction" or "borderline." We were afraid to pursue the subject. If she

knows her condition, it is her secret. Peeks into her
private world are rare; her invisible shell many times still
buffers her feelings. She shares vacations and the Christmas holidays at home with us, but after a few days she is
ready to return to her friends and the activities at the
home. She writes letters to some of the girls and buys
gifts for others.

The cost of presents or items Joy wants for herself is
of no concern. If an item is expensive, her standard reply
is, "What's the diff?" But she is easily distracted and soon
settles for a reasonably priced article and is excited and
anxious to wrap it in pretty paper and ribbon. Choosing
the just-right card to accompany any gift is a slow process, as Joy reads the sentiments carefully to be sure they
express her true feelings.

Last year Joy made my birthday card, similar in
appearance to several she hand-lettered as a child. "To
someone whom I love more than anyone else. I hope you
have many more. God bless you Always. Here is your
cake in modified form. Ha! Ha!" The round cake she drew
to illustrate the card was decorated with flowers and
another greeting, "Happy Birthday, Mom" and fifty-eight
marks for candles. The card, on lined yellow tablet paper,
is a treasured item in my desk!

I know deep within my heart that both Joy and God
have forgiven us our many mistakes and the cruel results
of our ignorance in handling her problems. But I doubt
Joy has totally forgotten the hurts she endured. They do
not sting or sear now as they must have at the time. We
rarely refer to those unhappy days. Occasional glimpses
into her memory bank cast temporary clouds over the
sunny disposition she has today. Somehow she under-

stands and loves us as we love her.

Why she was handicapped is of little importance now, and I no longer ask, "Why *Joy?*" Neither do I ask, "*Why,* Joy?" when she does something unsuitable or makes some illogical remark. The many whys of Joy are fewer now that we do not cast about for a scapegoat!

My "why" was an exclamation of pride last autumn as we walked through her favorite park, scuffing the brilliant fallen leaves and listening to them crunch under our feet. Some sailed through the nippy air and others skittered over still-green grass. "Jack Frost had his paint box here," I said, smiling at Joy. She corrected me. "It's the chlorophyll in the sap. I read about that in Sherri's dad's book. There ain't no Jack Frost—but I like to think there is."

Habit tempted me to correct her grammar, but before I could do so she rephrased the sentence herself. She grinned and shrugged her shoulders, "What's the diff?" Then we hugged and kissed, and I looked at the leaves in a brand new way.

I also see my beautiful daughter differently now that the double blindfold of ignorance and pride has been removed. Our choice of her name seems even more appropriate now than it did thirty-four years ago today.

Time has dulled the stabs of unpleasantries and honed my awareness of the beauties of everyday life. Our personal cloud cover had a silver lining all the time, but Jerry and I were slow to see it. I know that it takes two peaks to form one valley, and that our pattern is now complete.

Joy and Jonathan, Jerry and I are happy and comfortable with our lives. Placement separated us physically but reunited us spiritually. It was a horrendous decision, which the Lord eased when he guided us to the home-away-from-home.

Once I stopped struggling and accepted God's will, trusting him implicitly, he led us upward and over the many stumbling blocks called "whys" to joy, in Joy, and to peace and happiness in him. He made possible a happy ending to this open letter to those who share life with their own Joys.

Recently on the return trip from our regular monthly visit to Joy, I saw a billboard with a succinct message which fits the situation: "God makes house calls." *God* was the "doctor" we had sought so long. His prescription was simple: Faith and trust in *his* love and guidance. The hymn which Joy still sings now and then held a truism for her. "Jesus loves me ... The Bible tells me so." Jesus *does* love her! And God loves her! She knew it all the time.

I should have listened to her more closely as she sang the childhood hymn. The Bible held the answers to our questions. James 1:2-4 said what I needed to hear. "Count it all joy, my brethren, when you meet various trials, for you know that the testing of your faith produces stead-fastness. And let steadfastness have its full effect, that you may be perfect and complete, lacking in nothing."